PRAISE FOR *BRAND LOVE*

"I am thrilled to endorse *Brand Love*. It is an absolute must-read for an[illegible] who wants to build strong, lasting emotional connections w[illegible] consumers. I found the book to be a valuable reso[illegible] framework for continuous human-centric brand ev[illegible] considering cultures and customer values as key ele[illegible] Michael's writing style and tone are some of my favo[illegible] [illegible]ook. She is a multicultural marketing thought leader, globa[illegible], and expert consumer who weaves her professional expertise with personal experiences alongside the latest research and compelling case studies, offering a perspective that is highly relatable, relevant, and exciting. What sets *Brand Love* apart is how Michael's own expertise and passion in the subject took me on my own personal journey of falling in love with the book. With each stage of 'The Eight Brand Love Stages,' my desire to implement these strategies grew. Overall, I highly recommend *Brand Love* to seasoned and up-and-coming marketers alike. It's a powerful and insightful book that will breathe new life into the way you think about engaging consumers through emotionally driven strategies."
Ashmi Elizabeth Dang, Vice President of Marketing and Communications, Wayfarer Studios

"Lydia Michael gets it and makes it easy for you too. Customers own your brand! Michael provides real-world stories from companies you know and love that demonstrate the importance of moving your customer relationship from transactional to brand love. *Brand Love* shows how to create a customer for life. Why else be in business?"
Ron Davis, loyalty and information technology executive

"There are many books about marketing, but *Brand Love* is unique. It not only puts on a pedestal the importance of emotional engagement in brand building, but it does so by emphasizing the critical need of addressing the multicultural perspective when doing so. With the world becoming more diverse every day, that is now an imperative for brand growth. And I love all the practical examples!"
Bill Duggan, Group EVP, Association of National Advertisers (ANA)

"*Brand Love* offers a deeply personal and relatable journey through the intricacies of building strong consumer-brand connections. The book touches upon essential frameworks and quickly steers the reader through impactful stories of how they can be applied. *Brand Love* reminds us of a world obsessed with AI and deep technologies in that the biggest challenge in business can only be addressed by thinking through first principles and acting from our hearts."
Roman Fernandez, Venture Architect, Evolvia

"Brand love is a powerful force. Lydia Michael's book delves into this topic, revealing why we create emotional ties to some brands and not others. If you want your brand to be loved, this book gets to the heart of the matter and shows you just how to do it."
Christophe Folschette, Founder & Chief Strategy Officer, Talkwalker

"This is the toolkit you need if you want people to fall in love—and stay in love—with your brand! As a marketing professional, I found the eight stages to achieving brand love incredibly relevant, impactful, and easy to follow. Lydia Michael's unique personal and professional background has armed her with a wealth of knowledge that shines through in each chapter as she shares countless examples and personal client experiences. Her focus on cultural nuances offers refreshing insights that any brand could benefit from. The 'Love Notes' absolutely stole my heart! These key takeaways at the end of each chapter are clear, concise, and actionable. This is a book you'll find yourself coming back to again and again as you continue to build your brand."
Ashley Franso, Senior Project Manager, Commonwealth McCann

"What's love got to do with it? Well, everything. Without brand love, businesses struggle to stand the test of time. 'Love,' however, is a soft and fluffy topic. Thankfully, Lydia Michael provides structure and rigor to how brands can ignite desire and fandom—mapping out a path for the eight stages of brand love with tips and inspiration for each step of the process. Readers will be left reflecting on where their own brand sits on their journey for love and how they can continue to drive deeper connections."
Jon Freshwater, Client Partner, AKQA

"In her first book, *Brand Love*, Lydia Michael cements her position as a prolific thought leader with an expansive knowledge of global markets and the human psyche. She thoughtfully takes us through the journey of the 'The Eight Brand Love Stages' that is the tried and true roadmap for any size business to create

meaningful consumer-brand connections that will result in brand loyalty. What's most delightful about her observations is the insight she provides, stressing the importance of connecting with key demographics and multicultural consumers as well as supporting diverse and minority-owned brands."
Joya Harris, VP, Strategy & Creative, DCI Marketing (Marmon/Berkshire Hathaway Company)

"*Brand Love* not is not only an informative how-to, but it is substantive in its delivery on the importance of building a brand that resonates with customers, how it's good for business and why it's essential for long-term growth. This book is a must-have guide for any marketing and brand professional."
Shikha Jain, Partner, Simon-Kucher

"Lydia Michael has given us a fresh take on a topic that can easily become a marketing cliché: 'brand love.' Combining insights into emotional and rational drivers, she offers a framework for building brand connections that last. Peppered with practical examples and helpful chapter love notes, her book is a great read for marketing practitioners, no matter your level of experience."
Steve Keller, Sonic Strategic Director, Studio Resonate, SXM Media

"Lydia Michael makes a compelling case as to why brands should strive to build meaningful emotional connections with consumers. She clearly lays out the stages of building brand love, in a way that makes it accessible to a wide audience, from students to career-long marketing professionals. In an increasingly competitive market, brand identity is more important than ever, and as Michael points out, consumers are drawn to brands that reflect aspects of their own values and represent the multiple dimensions of their identities. This book is filled with valuable insights for anyone who is looking to develop brand recognition, build customer loyalty, increase social impact, or build company culture from the ground up. It's also a wonderful resource to help guide young professionals as they cultivate their own personal brands in the early stages of their careers. Well-organized, thoughtful, and inspiring!"
Heba Khadre, digital customer experience associate

"*Brand Love* goes where no other marketing material has gone to date, providing a manual for professionals to strengthen consumer bonds and produce brand champions and loyalists. Lydia Michael does an incredible job tapping into her extensive professional experience to provide readers with tangible insights and examples, and she follows these with actionable takeaways for all to use."
Shahbaz Khan, Global Director, Flagship Social Media, Nike

"Filled with personal anecdotes and marketing insights, *Brand Love* analyzes the core aspects of building and growing a successful brand that consistently connects with customers. Readers will love this book. The featured stories are exciting, the eight-stage brand love model and studies are relevant, and Lydia Michael's concise and digestible writing style is highly engaging."
Gabriela Klewenhagen, Digital Marketing Manager, SAP

"Lydia Michael does a fantastic job showing how an investment in a brand can build trust, loyalty, and drive real business results. The relevant examples in this book make it a must read for any professional who is serious about building an everlasting brand that adapts and engages with diverse audiences."
Fares Ksebati, Co-founder and CEO, MySwimPro

"For an organizational psychologist, one of the most important concepts to understand about whether people will engage is how connected they feel. Whether it's with a company, coworkers, or a brand, we engage where we feel we belong. *Brand Love* guides us through the steps to inviting others to be a part your brand—a place where they feel welcome and will want to stay. We invest heavily into presenting our brand in a way that will interest our customers. This book helped me to see that my brand is owned by my customer—they decide what my brand is—and how to positively influence that perception. *Brand Love* quickly establishes its own brand that is easy to fall in love with."
Tracy Maylett, CEO, DecisionWise, organizational psychologist, professor, and bestselling author of *Swipe: The Science Behind Why We Don't Finish What We Start*

"Lydia Michael presents a refreshing and digestible look into gaining the trust of customers that leads to a love of your brand in a world where people are demanding more than ever from the brands they consider buying. A must-read for marketers aiming to stay ahead of the curve."
Chioke McRae, Associate Director, Strategic Planning Analyst, Leo Burnett

"I enjoyed reading *Brand Love* because it brought to my attention different ways to engage with customers. Looking at brands ranging from huge and multinational, to small and local companies, emphasized how these ideas can be put into play across companies of vastly different sizes, budgets, and product lines. I also appreciate the push to utilize all five senses when connecting with customers, and the emotional ties that form as a result."
Kevin Peterson, Co-founder, Cocktail Scientist and Nose, Sfumato Fragrances, Castalia

"I'm very impressed with the attention to detail, the incorporation of inclusion and multicultural marketing, as well as real life examples to help put all the content into perspective. Inclusion in branding is getting more and more attention, and Lydia Michael is by far the best subject matter expert I've met. In this book, I especially love the 'Love Notes' at the end of the chapters that effectively summarize the most impactful points. *Brand Love* should be used by any company or organization looking to effectively create a brand that wants to be inclusive and create a lasting impact!"
Taharah Saad, Executive Director, Arab American Women's Business Council

"The framework introduced here is parsimonious, and Lydia Michael skillfully uses the complete canvas to paint the picture so that one can see how it is applicable to a wide variety of situations. It is elegant in its simplicity. Drawing upon work with clients and a body of evidence from a number of studies, she introduces 'The Eight Brand Love Stages' and provides the reader with the scaffolding to both comprehend and construct strong ties between consumers and the brands they will love. While many are familiar with the contours of customer relationship management, few are well versed in the rational and emotional underpinnings of the relationship, and this exposition regarding the drivers of brand love ensures that we will not overlook the sometime subtle, but always critical influence of these factors."
Jeff Stoltman, Director, Entrepreneurship and Innovation Programs, Mike Ilitch School of Business, Wayne State University

"In order to thrive in today's competitive environment, one must familiarize themselves with Lydia Michael's *Brand Love*. This book offers guidance on creating an intimate bond between a brand and consumers, which is integral for a successful business. What I love most about this book is its real world, global examples that make the concepts in this book easy to follow. Michael simplifies what brand love actually means while simultaneously segregating the 'Brand Love Drivers' into emotions versus logic or the right versus left side of our brains. With its emphasis on identifying your brand's 'why,' the book delivers an essential roadmap for business owners striving to cultivate long-lasting customer relationships."
Dionne Vaz, Marketing Director, CoinDesk

Brand Love

Building Strong Consumer–Brand Connections

Lydia Michael

First published in Great Britain and the United States in 2023 by Kogan Page Limited

2nd Floor, 45 Gee Street
London
EC1V 3RS
United Kingdom

8 W 38th Street, Suite 902
New York, NY 10018
USA

4737/23 Ansari Road
Daryaganj
New Delhi 110002
India

www.koganpage.com

Kogan Page books are printed on paper from sustainable forests.

ISBNs

Hardback 978 1 3986 1130 6
Paperback 978 1 3986 1127 6
Ebook 978 1 3986 1129 0

British Library Cataloguing-in-Publication Data

A CIP record for this book is available from the British Library.

Library of Congress Cataloging-in-Publication Data
Names: Michael, Lydia, author.
Title: Brand love : building strong consumer-brand connections / Lydia Michael.
Description: London ; New York, NY : KoganPage, 2023. | Includes bibliographical references and index. | Summary: "The best brands evoke the emotions of their customers by tapping into their hearts and minds.Individuals connect with brands the same way they connect with people. As a marketer, it's your responsibility to cultivate that relationship with your consumers. In this book, marketing and brand strategist Lydia Michael breaks down the process of building culturally inclusive, long-lasting consumer-brand relationships. Brand Love describes how brands appeal to the emotions of their consumers and why everybody benefits when brands earn the love of their customers. The author explains what marketers need to do to make consumers fall for their brands. The book builds on in-depth brand interviews and insights from companies such as Huda Beauty, LEGO and Toyota. She also shares what she has learned through client work and her observations in multicultural settings. Offering insight into the use of emotional and rational drivers, she introduces a "brand love" model designed to inspire brand loyalty and advocacy. With emotional elements such as humanization, personalization and trust alongside rational elements like relevance, differentiation and innovation, the author highlights the best ways to create or reinforce brand love to help your organization remain profitable and a source of inspiration, even during challenging times. Whether you're a marketer for a big or small brand, Brand Love will show you how to capture the hearts of your customers"– Provided by publisher.
Identifiers: LCCN 2023017443 (print) | LCCN 2023017444 (ebook) | ISBN 9781398611306 (hardback) | ISBN 9781398611276 (paperback) | ISBN 9781398611290 (ebook)
Subjects: LCSH: Brand loyalty.
Classification: LCC HF5415.32 .M49 2023 (print) | LCC HF5415.32 (ebook) | DDC 658.8/343–dc23/eng/20230519
LC record available at https://lccn.loc.gov/2023017443
LC ebook record available at https://lccn.loc.gov/2023017444

Typeset by Integra Software Services, Pondicherry
Print production managed by Jellyfish
Printed and bound by CPI Group (UK) Ltd, Croydon, CR0 4YY

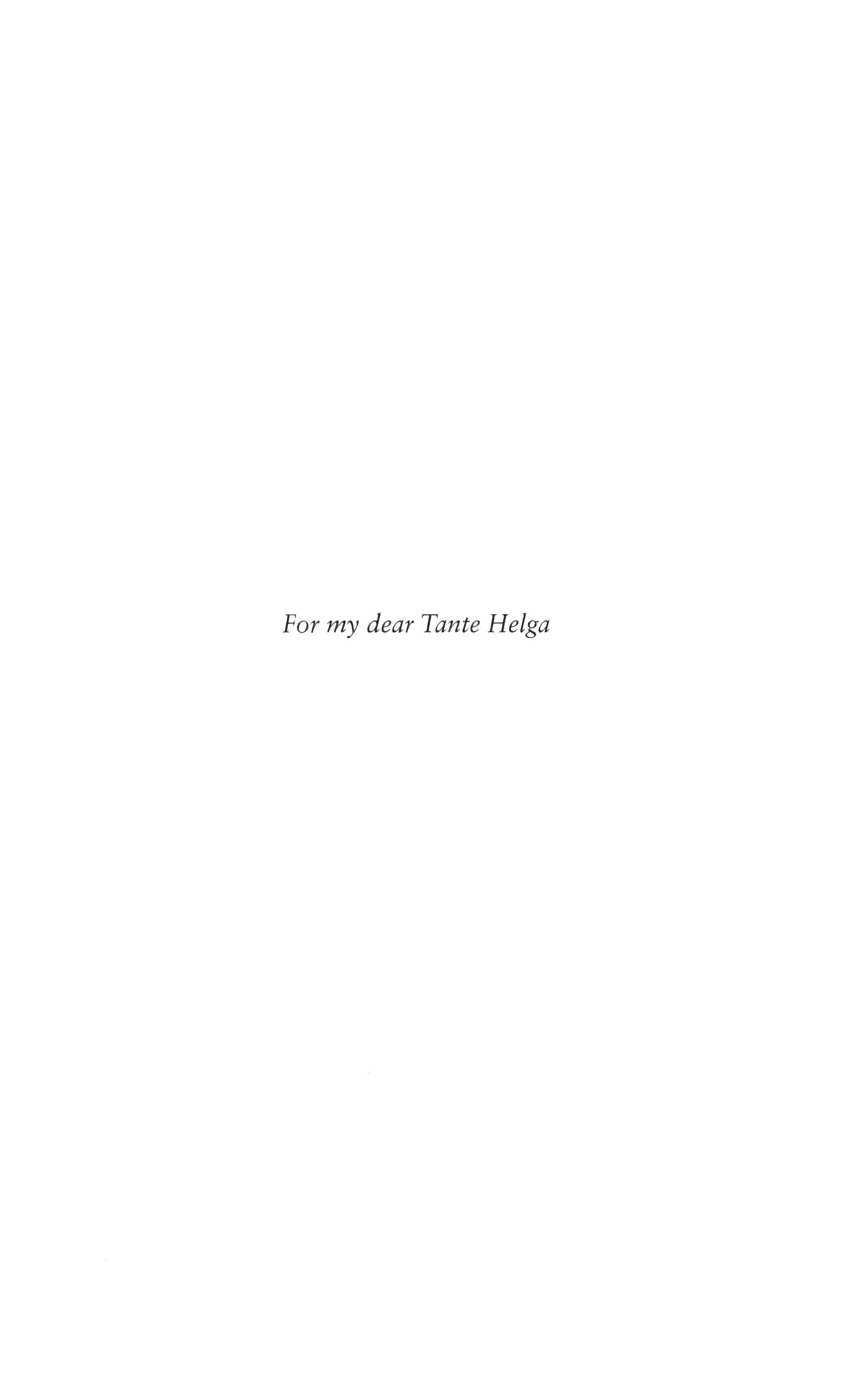

For my dear Tante Helga

"Life is full of little decisions—like white or brown rice."
Unknown

CONTENTS

PART THREE Rational drivers

PART FOUR Love reinforced

AUTHOR'S NOTE

This book is a true labor of love because it allowed me to share many of my experiences and thoughts on the marketing industry in a unique and creative way. Alongside my experiences, I include insights from client work from my own consulting firm, interviews with business owners, international brands, creative leaders, and marketers I spoke with specifically for this book, as well as research studies from notable firms globally. I also write about brands that are interesting, intriguing, and inspiring—ones I took note of over many years. Some will be relevant for years to come while others might be of less relevance as I wrote this book in real time. What is here to stay though, I'm sure, is the desire for consumers to connect with brands in deep, emotional ways.

At the core, brands do this by being human. Being human is a brand's biggest asset as consumers seek companies that go beyond transactional value and know how to laugh and cry with you, building meaningful connections. The truth is consumers want brands who think and act like them. Above all, they seek humanlike relationships. Many times, the brands who resonate with them are the ones consumers see themselves in and who position themselves to foster connections with people. What's important to realize is that for brands, the human side needs to be activated on a regular basis as people connect with the human side of brands. People also run the companies that consumers interact with, so they're innately human. For this reason, I chose to embrace my creative freedom by personifying brands throughout the book, referring to them as brands or companies *who* instead of brands or companies *that*.

It is my hope that this book will challenge your thinking and guide you, so that you can build and grow a brand who stands the test of time. My motivation was to write a book that addresses the ways in which brand love can be built with strategy and emotion. More than that though, I wanted to write a book that looks at brand love from a multicultural perspective, too. Why? Because we look at the world based on the way we perceive it, the way we see it. The importance of culture in marketing is relevant to consider. We base our consumer choices on our values and view the world based on the cultures we grow up in and that surround us. This affects our consumer behavior, attitudes, and lifestyle. Because of this, I reference brand examples across different cultures and markets to give you a glimpse into brand love in different, international contexts. After all, emotions are universal and travel through cultures and experiences in the same way brands do.

brand love (brænd ləv) NOUN

1. an emotional bond between a consumer and a brand.

2. a meaningful consumer-brand relationship that is driven by feelings of deep desire and affection.

3. a long-term connection with a brand that leads to customer loyalty and advocacy.

Introduction

We connect with brands the same way we connect with people. Similar to how we develop relationships with people in our personal lives, we shape these with our favorite brands. Whether on a website or in a store, consumers seek connection. This consumer-brand relationship is shaped over time and tested throughout the life of both the brand and the consumer. The most successful brands are the ones with emotionally engaged customers, the ones who know how to evoke emotion that translates into meaningful interactions time and time again. In the same way our ideal personal relationships are trustworthy, honest, and encouraging, so are people's perceptions of their favorite brands. If customers connect with brands the way they do with people, why wouldn't brands create themselves to be fully experienced and position themselves as worthy of falling in love with? For decades, brands like Patagonia, The LEGO Group, Toyota, and others that I talk about in this book, have been leading the way to brand love through emotional engagement with their customers. But can people truly fall in love with a brand?

What is brand love?

As a brand leader and marketer, I love using the lens of both to help me understand the link between brands and consumers as it relates to brand love. With this understanding comes emotional connection. With emotional connection comes engagement. And with engagement and the right level of trust comes loyalty that helps your business grow. Who doesn't want that?

My first job out of college in 2009 was with a Detroit- and Los Angeles-based artist relations and management firm and its independent record label we later created, where my role was to help guide artists and ventures from inception to growth. While spearheading global marketing and operations management efforts for five years, I worked closely with the team to market and manage Grammy-winning artists and their brands internationally. At the core, each one of these artists was their own brand—a personal brand that people connected with on an emotional level. Our artists understood that their success involved more than just writing or producing music that was well crafted while pulling all-nighters in the studio. It involved thinking deeply about who you are as a person, what you believe, and how you want to impact the world with your music and brand. Inevitably, once you achieve a certain level of success as an entertainer, it becomes difficult to detach your brand from your personal image. People simply see these artists as this very same person 24/7. Because of this, they have to serve as role models and feel a strong sense of responsibility whether they like it or not.

Seeing fans become obsessed with our artists from across the globe, tweeting them in Japanese, and patiently waiting for their arrival to do another jazz show in Tokyo, inspired me. I joined the next tour in Japan to represent the management firm and oversee press and marketing efforts onsite. The Japanese tweet turned into fans arriving early at the show, buying multiple pieces of available merchandise and music, taking pictures throughout the entire show, and singing along to every song in English, even when they didn't speak the language. As if that wasn't enough, they waited eagerly outside the green room to connect with the artists after the show. Throughout my time at the firm, I witnessed lots of admiration for many of our artists from fans globally and heard crazy stories, but all were unmatched to the level of brand obsession I came across in this part of the world. It was special and genuine. You know when you walk into a room full of people and you can just sense the good vibes and energy? The music wasn't the only thing that was mesmerizing—it was the all-encompassing experience of the audience, culture, food, and yes, even the staff who was into it. With every interaction, the artists delivered something that the fans loved, whether it was accessibility, gratitude, humor, or simply their talent. By traveling the world and therefore having such a detailed understanding of their audience, which is different from country to country, the artists knew exactly how to adjust their presence, message, and story for their brand to resonate authentically and emotionally from culture to culture. Every single time.

Emotions play a critical role in how we operate in our daily lives. Sometimes we're drawn to people or products for reasons beyond explanation; our gut feeling just tells us, "This is it." I can't count the number of times people have told me to trust that feeling—that intuition. It's this gut feeling that I've learned to trust over the years, both at work and in my personal life. Sometimes it can even feel out of character to gravitate toward certain brands or products based on who we think we are or want to be. Moments like this may be rare in our customer journey but they shouldn't be discounted because there's meaning behind everything we are attracted to.

To be successful though, we should consider both our feelings and our mind, allowing our emotional and rational side to guide us. The goal is to find a harmonic balance. Is the loyalty we seek in our personal lives any different than the loyalty we seek as customers with brands?

If you want to connect with someone on a deeper level, you might reveal something personal about yourself. Typically, this vulnerability is reciprocated. This is often because there is mutual trust and affinity between two parties when there's a connection. We want to be emotive and give people a reason to connect and share. Ultimately, we connect with people that we like and trust. We fall in love with brands in a very similar fashion. This is a concept called **brand love**. While conducting interviews with brand leaders for this book, several of them asked, "How do you define brand love?" Emotional marketing is nothing new, of course. The connection between marketing and psychology goes back decades, and brand love is a growing marketing strategy among agencies, consultancies, and brand marketers. At the time of writing and working on this book, there still isn't a widely recognized definition so I decided to offer my own at the start of this book. In fact, when you search "brand love" on Google you receive more than 3.5 billion results. The results on the first page of searches show a pattern of language that pops up such as "emotional connection," "loyalty and advocacy," "meaningful customer bonds," or "long-term relationship between customers and brands." All of these snippets of brand love are true. So, what does the concept of brand love entail?

Brand love is an emotionally strong, long-term consumer-brand connection that leads to loyalty and advocacy.

Why does B2C get all the love? What about B2B?

I want you to know that building a brand that people care about deeply doesn't require a big budget. And telling a good, powerful story that resonates doesn't either. Sometimes we're fooled to believe you need to have all this money or be a big company to create impact, but I've experienced the opposite to be true early on in my career. In fact, I believe this is what has allowed me to become more creative over the years. Small budgets demand more creativity and flexibility in utilizing existing resources. In similar ways, it also doesn't matter if you're B2C or B2B. The idea of emotional marketing can and should be applied in both segments.

In the marketing and brand practice, brand love continues to gain more popularity as a marketing strategy in the B2C segment. But what about B2B? I want to make sure to address both B2C and B2B early in this book because it's a question that continues to emerge every time I speak on the topic of brand love publicly. Last time I was speaking at a marketing conference, someone came up to me afterwards and asked how this could be applied to the work he does for an automotive supplier. He explained that he only deals with other businesses and has no interaction with customers directly but thinks this concept or strategy needs to be included in his work, too. Well, that's right. We can't assume that B2B is purely rational business. Other businesses can be customers, and these businesses are run by people too; people who make decisions and have emotions. It's easy to forget the B2B segment when a lot of research and examples in the marketplace focus on B2C. What's important to remember is that regardless of B2C or B2B, people and their interactions with one another matter. In the same way that B2C brands can connect with their customers by creating emotional bonds, so can B2B brands. Both go beyond rational factors, beyond reason.

According to a 2021 study from Porsche Consulting called "The Secret of Love": "Although B2B buying is often treated as an activity influenced solely by logical factors such as product features or cost-benefit analyses, in reality the process is driven by the same complex mix of gut feeling, emotions, and reason that drives all human decisions."[1] I'm sure others would argue that sometimes, especially in business, certain decisions are purely logical and rational and that including any sort of emotion isn't a good idea. This can relate to a more internal work environment but when we're dealing with customers, even as it relates to B2B, emotions should be considered in the same way. Why? We're still dealing with people here, remember? That's why. We're nurturing relationships that in some ways are accompanied by emotions. In addition to building this emotional bond between a business and another business, it's also possible to highlight this connection by showcasing the positive feelings your customers, that is other businesses, have for you. When a brand is loved, it can impact a customer's willingness to pay less attention to price, promote the brand through word of mouth, and overall show more loyalty. That is, as long as a brand is worth investing in and people feel like they're getting value in exchange for their money. Management guru Tom Peters said it right: "In an increasingly crowded marketplace, fools will compete on price. Winners will find a way to create lasting value in the customer's mind."[2]

Explaining the book

Before we dive into the first chapter, I want to explain the structure of this book. The book begins with the foundational elements of brand love. This section focuses on the relevance of brand love in the consumer-brand world and covers the basis of brand love and consumer desire. From there, we explore the ways in which many brands foster self-identification, self-reflection, or a sense of belonging. On a deep level, you forge stronger emotional bonds when a consumer identifies with your brand or product. I share "The Eight Brand Love Stages" and the "Brand Love Drivers" to take you on a journey of how to unlock the power of brand love based on the eight stages and emotional and rational drivers I introduce respectively.

The second part of this book focuses on the emotional drivers of brand love. From authenticity, purpose, sustainability, trust, personalization, humanization, and nostalgia, brands have a lot to check off their list if they're serious about building strong connections with customers for the long run. I introduce these drivers in a specific order. As it relates to emotional drivers, *being authentic* to your mission and purpose is at the core because it's something that you have to "be" before you can move on to drivers that describe actions you "do" such as *building trust*. When every single one of these drivers is present to build this deep relationship, you're on a better journey to achieving brand love.

While there are brands who are synonymous with one of these drivers, especially because they live and breathe one of these at minimum, the ones who embody the most drivers are best equipped to succeed. When we think of purpose-driven marketing, Patagonia and Ben & Jerry's are often some of the first brands to come to mind. When we think of brands who have captured the hearts of their customers for so long and create moments of nostalgia, brands like The LEGO Group often come up. These companies check off other drivers too to build strong emotional connections in the buyer's journey, but they still are known to the public as representing one driver so deeply that you can consider them almost synonymous with their brand names. In fact, many of the brands I discuss in this book likely represent multiple drivers. Sometimes, I use the same brand across different chapters to highlight different drivers they focus on. It's also important to note that some drivers might be more relevant than others and without them, becoming a love brand can easily be out of the question. If, for example, a business is personalizing experiences with their customers but can't be trusted, what good is the personalization portion? Trust is obviously foundational here. It's fair to say that many of the drivers won't matter much if a brand doesn't know how to earn and keep the trust of customers. So, yes, the drivers hold different values if you break them down in detail.

Part Three of the book talks about the rational drivers such as brands being relevant, different, consistent, experiential, innovative, or convenient. These rational drivers are just as important as the emotional drivers I reference in Part Two and don't necessarily come after the emotional ones. In fact, none of these drivers happen in a specific order when it comes to emotional versus rational drivers. It's important to note that both of these should be top of mind at any moment in time because of how closely consumers and brands emotionally interact.

After I discuss the emotional and rational drivers, I bring the book to an end with Part Four by talking about how brands operate differently during difficult or challenging times in an effort to continue building emotional bonds with customers. With consumer behavior changing during such times, brand marketers must understand how to continue to appeal to people in a human way beyond transactional relationships and beyond reason. The end of every chapter features primary takeaways or "Love Notes" to summarize the chapter's key message.

Measuring brand love

It might seem tough to know how to measure brand love, but elements across channels, especially digitally and through AI these days, are helpful indicators to understand how human insights translate into emotions. Analyzing brand sentiment allows you to look at the positive and negative feelings or attitudes toward your business. For brand love measures, this can include positive engagement and feelings; words that mention feelings of emotion, happiness, passion, joy, or love; or simply keeping a brand relationship active in healthy ways that your customers can experience. Monitoring sentiment as I've seen companies do with a love score or love index is important regardless of whether you're operating in one or multiple markets. In this book, I don't talk about how brand love should be measured, but not because it's not important. This book is about the emotional and rational drivers that are required to drive brand love in an effective way.

In the end, brand love is all about understanding who your audience is and focusing on your customers. You should have a desire to understand the nuances and uniqueness of anyone you want to reach. Ask yourself, what is special about this individual and consumer group? When you know who they are and what they're all about, you can integrate this into your cohesive, long-term marketing and brand strategy. As you can imagine, brand love doesn't hit the bottom line immediately. It takes time as the brand evolves.

As we journey through the next 11 chapters, I ask that you begin to picture something you hold near and dear to your heart. Think of relationships with others. Think about a brand or product that you feel connected to. Which brands are your favorites and why? Which one brings out the best YOU?

I also invite you to think about the brand you represent. What are you selling at the core? Why do you exist as a brand? And how do you connect the dots by delivering what customers want and need while staying true to yourself?

As you think about these things, you will notice that there are undeniable parallels as it relates to feelings between the two: *people and people,* and *consumers and brands.* We succeed in relationships when we apply both our hearts and minds. Rarely is it enough to be guided by our emotions or rational thoughts alone. A healthy relationship exists when we apply both emotional and rational thoughts and feelings. Such relationships work in the same way with brands. Emotional and rational drivers don't work independently of one another, but together. A successful brand finds ways to be emotionally engaging while offering rational, or functional benefits, too.

So, why focus on "likes" when you can focus on love?

PART ONE
The brand love foundation

Why brand love? 01

Every time I travel internationally, I look for a bottle of Moschino's Glamour or Giorgio Armani's Emporio Armani Night Red. It sounds silly to look for discontinued items like these two iconic perfumes, but I still hold an ounce of hope that maybe one day I will stumble upon a duty-free store or a large outlet with one of these in stock.

The scent of perfume is one of the earliest and strongest memories I have. As a child growing up in Germany, I remember admiring my mom's perfumes and the bottle designs all lined up on her dresser. All of them captured my attention, from Rive Gauche by Yves Saint Laurent to Jil Sander No. 4. These very same scents and bottle designs still bring back warm and happy memories, transporting me to a special time and place. It's more than just a smell, it's about how it makes you feel—it's a memory. Products like these tell a story and if consumers don't understand it, they won't buy the product. As I've gotten older, the scents I've chosen for myself have evolved, but what remains are the strong emotions and memories that each one elicits. Now, my scents have become part of my personality.

Why does brand love matter?

Has your favorite brand or product ever been discontinued? How did you feel? When we love something we use, it becomes a part of our life that we can't see ourselves without; the brand fulfills a need. As customers, we feel a sense of attachment and loyalty to the item or brand who captures our hearts, and we are willing to do whatever it takes to stay loyal to the brand, even if there is a direct substitute.

After experiencing the loss of several discontinued products over the years including the aforementioned perfumes, I now stock up on products that I can't see myself without. That way, I have plenty in case they are discontinued down the road. This compulsion I feel to hoard my favorite products—something I know many individuals in my life do—serves to combat separation distress, a fear of losing the product and brand. You get used to a product, fall in love with it, rely on it, and when you wake up the next day, it's gone. Just like that. It feels worse than a breakup. It can make you feel like your life is ruined. The less a product is available, the more it becomes desirable. It's human nature—we want what we can't have.

I remember when my sister's favorite perfume was discontinued and completely rebranded in all aspects from the name to the scent formula as the brand wanted to consolidate under one brand name, aiming for a more consistent consumer experience. She said, "I don't know what to do without it. I've been using it for years, and it was my signature scent. I don't want to replace it with a new one." Seriously though. What option did she have but to go out and find a new perfume with the potential to become her favorite again? Companies decide to discontinue a brand or product for various reasons. Perhaps demand and sales are no longer strong enough or they need to rebrand. Maybe there's an issue with their supply chain, or the products simply don't support the brand's direction anymore. If you're lucky, a quick Amazon search may still show stock of your favorite product.

Emotions are instinctual. When people relate over a shared emotion, whether it's joy or sadness, it can build a stronger connection and foster loyalty. Similarly, people look for brands and companies who fit their lifestyles, values, and what they believe—brands they can connect with once they've demonstrated their value. When a brand understands what today's consumers desire, it can awaken emotions to start building brand love. As a brand, ask yourself: What drives consumers? What excites them? What do they love? What do they fear? According to Elisabeth Kübler-Ross, "There are only two emotions: Love and Fear. All positive emotions come from love, all negative emotions from fear. We cannot feel these two emotions together at the exact same time. They're opposites."[1] When it comes to consumers, it's safe to say they want to be aligned with brands who encourage positive energy and come from a source of love.

Customers who love a brand are loyal fans of it, and they will often recommend the brand to others through positive word of mouth, encouraging them to buy a product or service they've had a great experience with. This loyalty should be what all brands strive for. What brand or company doesn't benefit from unwavering consumer-brand relationships? Maintaining them is not easy, though, and requires mutual commitment and consistency. When brands experience difficult times or disruption across industries, they either benefit from strong, existing brand-consumer relationships or strengthen their emotional bonds with their customers by adapting to the evolving demands and changes. Understanding the voice of your customers is key, and you have to know what engages them throughout the consumer lifecycle.

You have to identify and analyze the problems and needs of your customers. Like a doctor who checks symptoms, diagnoses the problem, and provides a solution, it's your job as brand marketers to help clients identify the issue at hand, so that you can start looking for the solution, too. You need to put yourself in the shoes of your customers and deliver gains in response to the pain points they experience. Knowing what they need before they do is how you make the magic happen.

According to Talkwalker's 2021 Brand Love Story study, once you build this connection with them and truly understand their pain points and needs, these established consumer-brand relationships can often lead to the following:

- Price premium: Adults say they are willing to spend more on products and services from a brand they love, which means that a company can afford to charge a higher price that customers are willing to pay.[2]
- Brand loyalty: Customers are more likely to show loyalty toward a brand they have a strong relationship with, which many equate to loving a brand.[3]
- Brand advocacy: When customers love your brand, they are more likely to share it with and recommend it to others.[4]

Many beloved brands create strong, committed relationships where customers are willing to pay an above-average price, repurchase the brand, and share their positive experience with others. This encourages additional purchases and inspires loyalty in a way where price doesn't matter because of the quality and service consumers experience. In the Hispanic or Latino community, as experienced through a group of friends, people tend to connect with companies who promote strong experiences they can share with family and friends and sometimes even ask for their opinion to inform their purchase decision. The buyer's decision tends to be influenced by their friends and acquaintances. In the long run, this can create strong bonds between a customer and a brand. According to Nielsen's Diverse Intelligence Series 2021, the consumer buying power of U.S. Hispanics or Latinos, also sometimes referred to as Latinx, is increasing as they represent the largest racial and ethnic group in the U.S.[5] This Series from Nielsen also explains that brands and advertisers have started to take note and recognize the cultural untapped opportunities of this community that come with different experiences, perspectives, and expectations.[6] When this type of awareness turns into brand action with different cultural groups of people, engagement and growth become organic next steps for companies.

How to become a love brand

Not all brands are loved, but most would benefit from trying to be loved. The brands who focus on eliciting emotions tend to have better and deeper relationships with their customer base. Yes, there are rational or functional benefits that every brand offers and everyone needs, but these are not sufficient to build differentiation. Many functional benefits are category "must-haves" that relate to the functionality or specific performance of a product. On the other side are emotional benefits, such as sensorial drivers that connect to one of our five senses, offering the highest differentiation potential because they're strongly connected to emotions that can be expressed through tangible elements to build a powerful and differentiating proposition. It's the glue that keeps everything together (see Figure 1.1). So, what's the secret?

Figure 1.1 Brand Love Intersection

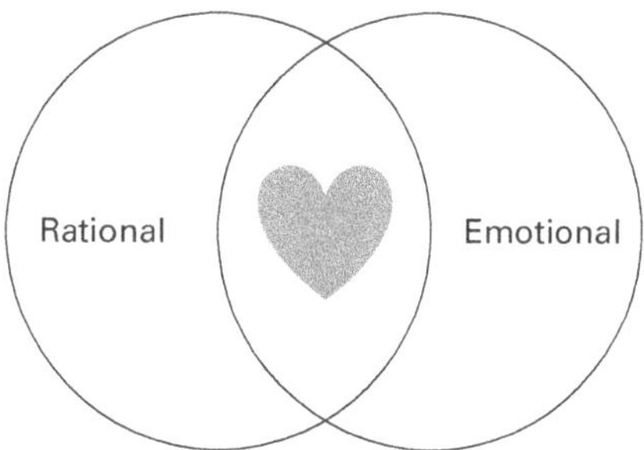

Based on my experience in working with brands and organizations throughout my career, I've recognized a pattern to achieve brand love that is made up of eight stages (see Figure 1.2). The 1986 triangular theory of love by psychologist Robert Sternberg that focuses on three different types of loves across the three scales of intimacy, passion, and commitment, also added to my inspiration. All of the eight stages I introduce have different brand and marketing activities attached to different stages. Some of these stages relate to the concept of brand desire while others relate to the concept of brand intimacy, or self-identification. Regardless, these stages must be tackled before the brand can move to the next stage with a consumer. Throughout the book, I share a variety of multicultural brand examples based on emotional and rational drivers that encompass the core of the book in parts two and three, and have a strong influence on these stages. Here's more detail about each stage of the brand love path.

You'll see that the first half of stages, that is awareness, familiarity, interest, and likeness, fall under the idea of brand desire that fuels growth. Being attractive to a certain group of consumers enables your brand to continue climbing the ladder. The closer your customer grows toward you, the more intimate the relationship becomes over time, leading to the second half of stages that encompass trust, attachment, love, loyalty, and advocacy. Throughout this journey as consumers develop a likeness toward a brand, there are typically elements of self-identification that develop. People feel a sense of their "self" reflected or mirrored in the brand. It's important to also note that once brand love is reached, it's not a result of only emotional or rational drivers. Brand love is a combination where emotional AND

Figure 1.2 The Eight Brand Love Stages

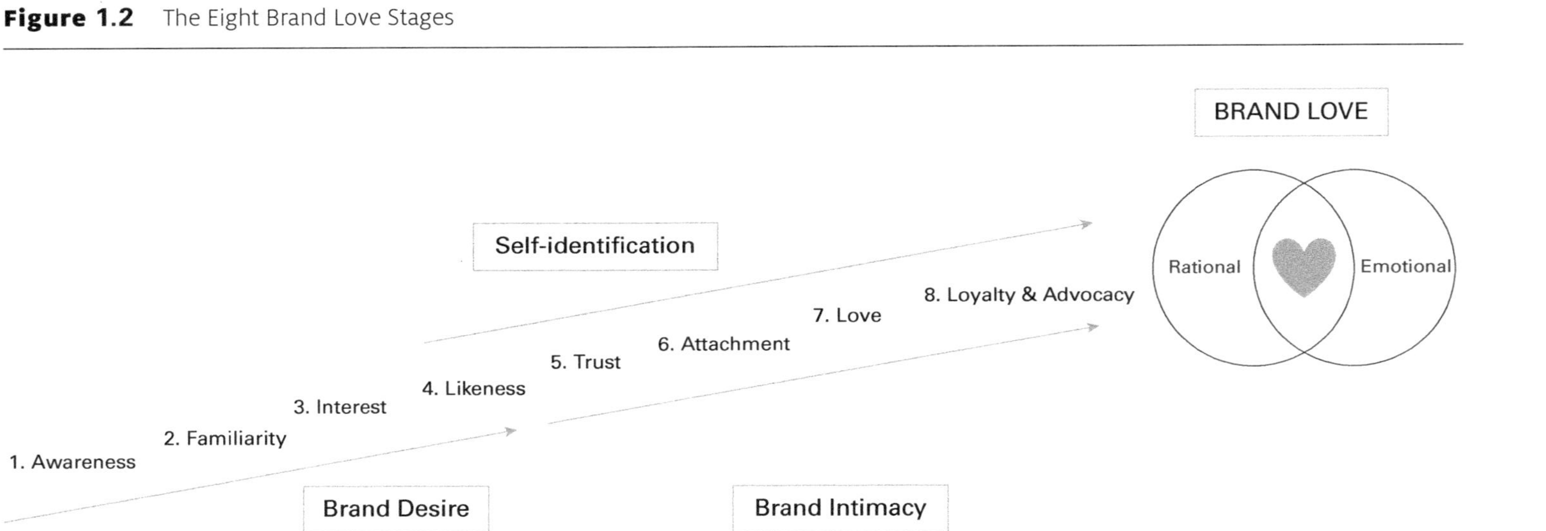

rational drivers meet. A customer is likely to experience multiple drivers simultaneously to develop a bond and grow close to a brand. In short, both are required for success. The more drivers are part of the experience, the better and stronger the consumer-brand connection will be.

The Eight Brand Love Stages

1. Awareness

People either know you or they don't. When working with new brands, the first question people ask is typically, "How can we let people know we exist?" If a customer hasn't yet heard of the brand, you have to work on creating brand awareness. People connect with brands the same way they connect with people, so why not think of your brand as a person instead of a business? What are the brand characteristics and values you want others to know? What is your WHY, your purpose? Can your brand laugh at itself or not? Sometimes it sounds easier said than done. It's not always easy to put together a powerful brand awareness strategy. Brands are also limited by their marketing budget. As someone who has worked with many small businesses, I know how important it is to maximize the impact and every dollar of your brand with a small budget. When you understand the core value you are offering to your target audience, the key is to find other brands and organizations in the community you can align those values with. It's easier to identify who can help your business, but what's crucial to understand is how you can help them as well. What value can you add? The relationships you build should be mutually beneficial to be long-sustainable. Once you've figured this out, you can start sourcing organizations who have a wide reach and require minimal budget, if any, to put you in front of their audience.

Ethnic chambers of commerce, for example, have proven to be a solution in working with businesses time and time again. Given that they have a cultural and diverse mix of people, they also have a steady membership base on average—an audience that's worth getting in front of. Attending events to introduce yourself and meet others is a no-brainer. You can also provide programming or a webinar about your product or service, guest-blog, host an event, or simply join as a member and be included in the email marketing efforts to be highlighted to other members. Some ethnic chambers actually don't require you to join as a member to receive their emails, but you can subscribe anyway. Others I have come across provide value to both members and non-members—in different ways of course. One chamber delivers value to non-members by offering event access, typically at a higher charge than for members, and provides opportunities to connect with companies and brands through annual events and business matchmaking. Creating this type of event awareness and offering value simultaneously helps you weigh your options for where you want to spend your dollars or time by joining such organizations in the community that can best serve your business and allow you to offer value, too. Ask yourself who can benefit best from the value you have to offer. Where can you create good opportunities? When I first started my business, I created relationships with almost every ethnic chamber by either becoming a member, attending regular events, hosting a webinar session, or moderating a panel. It was important to me that I created awareness early on to start building and nourishing these relationships in effective ways.

Besides this, you can advertise, sponsor events, produce a podcast, or create content, especially for your website to drive search engine optimization. Of all, the latter is easier than ever to authentically connect with your audience, whether through written or video format. As you can see, the path to creating awareness is endless. The more awareness you create for your brand, the more likely that your audience has enough time to process information about your brand and who you are. Just don't forget that consumers use multiple channels and devices to find out about new products and brands. Social media is one of them, and businesses tend to think they have to be present on every channel in existence. Far from it—but more about this in Chapter 9.

2. Familiarity

Brand familiarity can be more difficult to tackle than creating awareness. During this stage, people should understand who you are and what you're all about—it's more than knowing you exist. They need to understand what you're selling and ideally why, to make an informed decision in the stages to come that can strongly influence the purchasing process. This will in turn increase the likelihood of your brand being chosen over a competitor's brand. Being a familiar brand means you have to be recognizable and memorable based on how you choose to create awareness in the first place—how you choose to show up in the world. When familiar with your brand and product, the consumer is intrigued by your business and what you have to offer. They're fully aware and have likely shaped a perception of you at this stage. To generate interest beyond familiarity, it's not enough that your customer knows who you are—they need to know what you offer and why.

3. Interest

Remember, branding and marketing is not about you as much as it is about your customer who is the one making the decision and ultimately driving your sales. Now it's time to understand what they're all about, so they can pay attention to your offerings. This is the stage where more listening is needed. Listen to them, understand what they feel and what they say. If you're in the business launch stage, it's helpful to already have research available that you can tap into to best understand and categorize your target audience to appeal to their interest. This will require powerful research that allows you to go deep behind the need of the need as it relates to the customer. Qualitative research from one-on-one interviews or focus groups can provide the emotional insight you might need to truly understand more about your customer, and can generate interest in your brand. You want to position yourself as customer-centric and ensure the customer knows it's all about them. You're here to deliver a solution to their problem. Ultimately, your brand centers around your audience.

4. Likeness

Like leads to love, right? At least at some point. When people like your brand, it's usually because some part of it resonates with them. This is where self-identification takes shape as people see a part of themselves in brands they choose or find ways to identify on some level. When you've mastered the previous stage to generate interest in your business based on what you've identified as your target audience's wants and needs, likeness is a natural follow-up to this. If, as a brand, you're doing what your customer is looking for and are doing so in an authentic and genuine way, you're moving in the right direction.

5. Trust

This is the stage where brand intimacy begins to form. As customers, we trust brands the same way we trust our friends and family. When we like and trust someone, we are more likely to do business with them and show loyalty over the long term, but the opposite can also be said. This loyalty affects the value of the brand, the brand equity, which is also affected by other factors from how well the brand is perceived (or not, which would then result in negative brand equity) to how much awareness exists about it. According to the 2021 Trust Barometer® Special Report by global communications firm Edelman, "trust" is the new "brand equity"[7] and once trust is broken, it's difficult to earn it again. We like to connect with people and businesses who reflect their words with actions. Gen Z is extremely particular about brands they engage with and want to trust brands to do the right thing. Brands have to ensure they are following through with their promises to build and keep the trust of their customers.

6. Attachment

Emotional connection between brand and person really begins here. Brand attachment makes it easier for a customer to interact with your brand because you've given them enough reason to want to connect. You've shown them that you value them. At the same time, they're tied to something that uniquely distinguishes you from others in a way that gives them satisfaction. By continuing to embrace your difference and uniqueness, you can stay relevant to your customers' lives every step of the way. By staying true and honest to your brand and what you offer, customers will continue to find a reason to stay close to you.

7. Love

This is the destination on the path to brand love that some brands achieve more easily than others. Customers have a clear preference for a brand at this stage and don't put much thought into the cost of the product. In fact, they're willing to pay a high price because they know what they can expect when purchasing the product or service, or when engaging with the brand. The value proposition at this stage is so clear. In the early stages, customers might switch to a different product and not

the drivers ideally happen throughout the stages and consumer lifecycle. It's possible that one or multiple drivers can influence another driver, too. Emotional drivers such as trust, inclusion, and authenticity can drive the customer experience. Experience is listed in the rational category but can result in being emotional when driven by such emotional drivers.

Starting in Chapter 2, I introduce one of the emotional drivers of the "Brand Love Drivers," brand desire, and how it impacts the journey to brand love. The chapters following that will detail additional emotional and finally, rational drivers toward the end with different ways you can put brand love to work, even during challenging times.

Consumer behavior and psychology research shows that we, as individuals, are the average of the five people we surround ourselves with the most.[10] The people you spend time with shape who you are as they determine what conversations dominate your attention and what behaviors you are continuously exposed to. Eventually you begin to think and behave like them, which can have an impact on your success or failure in life to a certain extent. I know, that sounds far-fetched, but the point is that some people hold us back while

Figure 1.3 Brand Love Drivers

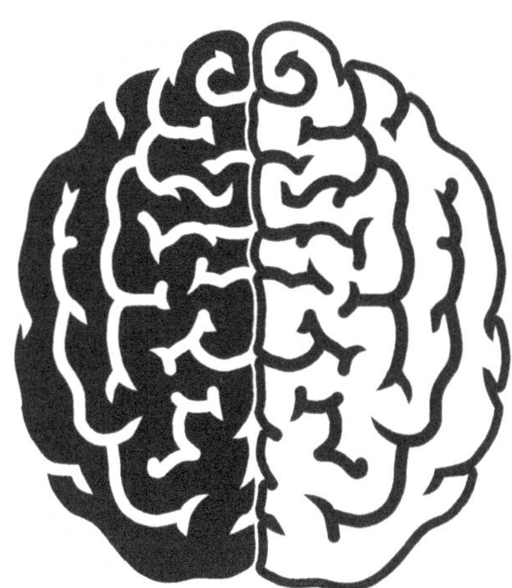

others propel us forward. What about the brands we use? Are we an average of the five brands we use the most? Is this linked, too? If this were the case, it would hold true that we have to choose brands as carefully as we choose our friendships and relationships.

Love Notes

1. **Consider "The Eight Brand Love Stages" model**
   The brand love journey is made up of eight stages to reach the pinnacle of brand love. When people love a brand, they are more likely to stick around, remain loyal, and turn into brand champions.
2. **Use emotional and rational drivers**
   The "Brand Love Drivers" include both emotional and rational drivers to help you build a successful and long-lasting consumer-brand relationship. You shouldn't choose one or the other but rather use them together.
3. **Strive to build consistent connections**
   People look for brands and companies who fit their lifestyles, values, and what they believe. They want brands they can connect with, so strive to foster consistent and emotional connections by understanding who you want to reach and engage.

Brand desire and intimacy

02

Before I dive into brand desire, let's go back to the concept of a brand. When new clients approach my team and I at Blended Collective, they often ask us if we can just create a quick logo... as if that's all there is to "branding." This is where our education starts.

A brand is meant to capture much more than what the consumer first sees, which is the visual identity. In short, a logo doesn't equate to a brand. Of course, the visual identity is utterly important as it encompasses the logo, typography, color palette, and other visual design elements, but this is only the start of the brand journey. If you get it right from the start, it can serve you well for the life of your brand. Branding also focuses on the customer experience, of which the visual identity is only one part. I'm not trying to downplay the importance of branding or creative design here but as a brand, you should ask yourself what your brand stands for early on in the process. If your brand were a person, what would it look, feel, sound, smell, or maybe even taste like? What would its character be? This is one of my favorite questions to ask when we kick off projects with our clients. It's a deep question that helps me understand someone's approach to their brand. The visual identity is informed by the foundation of what the brand stands for and what core values it holds, so we start the process by diving into deep brand exercises and research with our clients to start the branding journey, developing a brand who is special and desired by people for decades to come.

Your brand is owned by your consumer

A brand is the entire experience across all consumer touchpoints. Despite your intentions, efforts, and the time you spend to develop your brand identity, the brand image in the end is controlled externally by your customers and everyone else. Yup, you read this right. The essential difference between brand identity and brand image is the perspective—the perception. The brand identity is controlled by the brand owner, but a brand's image is owned by the consumer. The ways in which consumers see their environment, including brands, is quite subjective. To some individuals, a brand may look one way and to others, a completely different way. As an example, I consider the Ralph Lauren brand classy and timeless. Others might perceive it differently. Either way it goes, consumers perceive brands based on their own history of experiences, which shapes their brand opinions and the external brand reputation that many come to know over time.

How is your brand perceived by the public? What is at the heart of your brand image? Do people feel your brand is desirable? To successfully brand your business, your goal should be to ensure that the brand identity you develop is what consumers perceive as such because the only thing that matters is perception. As we develop brands, we strive to create a brand identity that reflects who the brand truly is—and in some cases it translates from who the founder is. You have to ask yourself, what is my brand about and why does anyone need it? By looking on the inside and discovering your values and beliefs, you start to put all these things together and develop a vocabulary and brand language—all of this becomes your brand personality. Your brand encompasses elements such as your mission, your vision, and your purpose at the very core. Your values entail what your company believes and stands for. These values are then used to create the visual identity to bring the entire brand to life and activate it in different ways. The brand image, on the other hand, encompasses all brand associations, emotions, and opinions people can have about your brand. Sometimes the two terms are used interchangeably but they represent different things. To close the gap between the two and ensure that your brand identity and brand image align, you have to do it through brand positioning.

Brand positioning describes the way consumers perceive a brand to be unique and different relative to competitive offerings—an effort that takes years. I provide an example of how to position a brand using water brands in Chapter 9, but for now, as you think about the position you want to create in the marketplace, you should consider questions such as: What conceptual place do you want to own in your consumer's mind? When and how do you effectively develop a brand positioning strategy that will continue to allow your brand to be relevant as well as distinct, resulting in increased brand value overall? And why does it matter? When you understand your customers' pain points and challenges with the gains that you offer in response, you can position your brand at every stage of their lifecycle to ensure that your brand is perceived as something they need, something that can't be fulfilled or delivered by a competitor—at least not in the way you're doing it. Think about many of the Apple products such as the iPod or iPad that many customers didn't know they needed or desired until they were told so. Or the skincare mini fridge that my 13-year-old cousin Brooklyn was convinced she needed to store and cool her beauty products for best effect.

I wouldn't say it's about selling us products we don't need, but more about creating a need for something that didn't exist before in a clever way that is mutually beneficial. Or addressing an unrecognized need that went previously unfulfilled. Something that might even outshine the competition. Do you recall a time when you discovered a product that made you feel like you'd been waiting for it your whole life? Like your life would never be the same again? A product that fits into your life so well that you don't even know what it was like to live without it? That's the type of desire brands should aim to create. A feeling of, "I need you and I can't live without you." I know at least for me, when I fall in love with a product, I will find a place for it in my life.

On this same customer journey, though, the experience can have an unfavorable result. The frustrations and pain we experience as customers may not be the same and can depend on the reason for the consumer-brand interaction. Does it depend on who seeks out whom? When a company puts something out there that catches the attention of us customers, we are the ones to choose the brand. On the other hand, when we're in the market looking for something, we go into the world to find the brand or product that's going to provide what we need. If we consciously and intentionally seek out a brand and later realize that the brand isn't what it's portrayed to be, feelings of disappointment can develop. We might doubt our own choices and be more critical of them because we think we should have known better. This is a feeling known as cognitive dissonance, where two ideas or behaviors conflict with one another. As humans, we want to limit this feeling of discomfort that comes from conflicting ideas. We do what we can to either limit the amount of new information we take in or learn to cope and accept the "new" truth.

Build your brand around impact

At my firm, I once worked with Mayfield Athletics,[1] an innovative sports equipment company with a passion to enhance safety and functionality for players of all ages. They wanted help with positioning an emotional and impactful value proposition through content creation from the start. S.A.F.E.Clip, one of their products, is an advancement in facemask clip design to replace standard clips installed on a football helmet at the factory or refurbisher. As scientifically proven at various third-party accredited laboratories across the country, S.A.F.E.Clip effectively reduces impact by up to 35 percent. Regardless of age, size, or athletic ability, the product is designed to fit almost every helmet and facemask combination on the market to help make football a safer game for all. One key target audience for the brand is parents, especially moms, whose children play football, as parents are keen on keeping their children safe when playing sports. Proven difficult to reach and capture, I was tasked to find engaging and impactful ways to attract parents' attention and desire to the brand's relevant product.

Using one of our firm's marketing strategy frameworks for this type of work, I recommended and developed the idea of attaching emotional attributes to the product to create a strong connection between the customer and brand. Stories can activate the parts of the brain that convince someone they are experiencing the story for themselves. An emotionally charged story in a content marketing campaign can make customers feel happy and ensure they have memories of the brand that will stick with them for a while. The result of the story is to prove that the product will create safety, happiness, and peace of mind for parents, hence pushing strong desire and relevance for the product. To push parents to act, I recommended that the content should be focused on overcoming feelings of fear and urgency to protect the children from concussions and other sports injuries. The key here is to help parents understand that they need the product because without it, they increase their child's potential to get injured during their sports.

Fear is a very powerful element of emotional marketing to approach with caution. When promoting a product, focus on eliminating fear by displaying the relief and safety that comes with the product. These feelings can be evoked through ads, video marketing, imagery, and other digital campaigns, resonating on an emotional level to create a strong connection between the product's purpose and the child's safety, pushing price to become a secondary factor in the decision-making process. When there is safety, there is a strong emotional pull, so the value proposition of the product can be built around this by creating impactful content. When doing so, the customer is encouraged to buy into the brand's purpose and value, which goes beyond selling the product. Emotional marketing tells a story that connects audiences with brands and products in personal and human ways. Parents have strong feelings about their child's safety and hence have a strong desire to protect them from sports injuries. An emotional story across multiple customer touchpoints supports the product's ability to create safety, happiness, and peace of mind for parents and children alike, ultimately increasing product sales for the company.[2]

Brand positioning strategies like this can help keep a brand relevant and profitable by improving the perceived value and competitive advantage of what they have to offer. Once developed and implemented effectively, the result is a customer perception, which allows brands to compete and therefore have a market advantage in the long term. It's not necessary to create something new and different, but rather to try to connect what already exists in the consumer's mind. Depending on the type of brand you have, different elements may be of more importance. For a restaurant, the physical space plays a significant role in how the brand is designed, while for a digitally based business, the website and social media elements are the key focus. Any business that has both a physical and digital presence requires a holistic brand experience where at all consumer touchpoints the brand is viewed as part of the same brand ecosystem.

When I built Blended Collective in 2017, I established core values of authenticity, culture, and diversity. In this order. I remember being in a meeting a few years later after our brand was up and running and someone pointing out that our core values are always mentioned in this same order: authenticity, culture, and diversity. Deep inside, I was so excited that someone externally recognized the importance of this order besides our own team. Why? Because the order mattered. A while later, I also heard one of our multicultural advisory board members refer to our core values as "ACD" when we were recording a promotional video for our company. He said, "Authenticity, culture, and diversity. That's the best way I can remember it." What might seem like a minor detail to some, is key in how my team and I position our brand to create impact. To hold true to these values, we've created different ways to manifest these in our daily activities and bring them to life. To reflect authenticity, for instance, we insist on only using photos of real people doing real things throughout all our marketing. Whether it's a presentation, marketing collateral, or website, we use authentic photos that we capture with photographers—no stock images whatsoever.

So, when we hosted a Speaker Event Series around multicultural marketing and diversity, equity, and inclusion, we captured real-time content of our audience at these events. It's content that we use for all of our marketing needs. The series featured creative and business talent extending across cultures and industries to highlight authentic, cultural, and diverse stories. The event organically provided a platform for industry experts to share their experiences, knowledge, and thought leadership. It also offered the audience an authentic voice to share their perspectives, forming new relationships and culturally relevant discussions in the community. These discussions included speakers from Ford Motor Company, General Motors, LinkedIn, Pandora (part of SiriusXM), Quicken Loans, and many more. Capturing this authenticity, culture, and diversity at our events, we found that this best reflects the community we engage with. Being intentional in how we continue to bring these core values to life is crucial to make the right impact.

Additionally, the value of culture is reflected in all our work throughout as we aim to integrate cultural elements into a client's marketing journey, whether it's about reaching a certain type of cultural group or demographic. With diversity as part of our values, this shows not only in the type of businesses and clients we work with or for, whether it's a minority-owned or women-owned business, but also in the diversity of many other factors such as diversity of thought, education, professional background, and more. This is how we, as a brand, can offer value beyond purely our services—with this community arm. Our brand extends into the community by bringing these multicultural backgrounds together through our services. Creating a space for an increasingly diverse group of people who want to come together to share their thoughts, experiences, and knowledge but also learn from each other by recognizing both their similarities and differences, is important to us.

We've given our community a reason to become a part of what we were building early on as we were growing the brand and nurturing these relationships. I remember event attendees would come up to us after an event, inspired by the program we had put together and the speakers we had sourced to connect in a unique way, asking how they could be a part of what we were building and whether we had a membership they could join. That's right. People wanted to pay us money to be a part of what we were building because they were that passionate about it. Even without a reason to hire us as a marketing and branding consultancy to work with, they wanted to be involved because they believed in what we stood for at our core—beyond our service offerings as a consulting firm.

Impact is a crucial element that can be used as a launching pad for brand desire. Throughout my career, I've focused on creating impact and desire for brands. One of them includes a project in Germany.

The relaunch of L'Oréal Germany's Garnier Fructis

In 2016, I was working at L'Oréal Deutschland (Germany) as part of my MBA International Management program. I had been assigned to the product marketing team with the brands *Garnier Fructis* and *Whole Blends* (*Wahre Schätze* in the German market), the mass market hair care brands under the cosmetics brand of French heritage. Some of my daily tasks included analyzing weekly market trends, competitors, digital and point-of-sale performance targets. On a larger scale, the team and I had agreed to center the topic of my master's thesis on a real-life project that required more research and recommendations during my time there. After brainstorming ideas, the decision was made that I was going to focus on the first rebrand in the German market of Garnier's brand Fructis, the green range of shampoo bottles known for its fruity scents, perceived as dynamic, carefree, and fun.

As a sucker for brands, I was excited to work on such a relevant and national relaunch. But the key question was, how can we create a successful love brand by re-launching a brand in the German hair care market that is desirable? I quickly found myself diving deep into studies, planning and hosting creative workshops with influencers to gain consumer insights, researching the concept of brand love while meeting with cross-functional colleagues across various brands and categories such as skincare, make-up, hair care, hair color, fragrances, and others, including hygiene. My brain was like a sponge during this time... I couldn't learn enough. The goal was to develop visual, content, pricing, and digital marketing strategies after analyzing market data, organizing focus groups, and collecting insights based on key performance indicators (KPIs). L'Oréal Germany, responsible for adapting and localizing more than 36 brands in the German market,[3] includes a global brand portfolio with subgroups of Consumer Products, L'Oréal Luxe, Professional Products, and Active Cosmetics.[4] Many would be surprised to learn that brands such as Essie, Giorgio Armani Beauty, Yves Saint Laurent, and Shu Uemura, are under the umbrella of L'Oréal.[5] With so many multicultural brands under one roof, the brand seems to understand well how diverse beauty is and how it needs to be adapted in a globalized setting to function successfully across various markets.

The Garnier Fructis brand, specifically the green product range, aims to enhance the consumer-brand relationship with a core target of 18- to 49-year-old consumers in the German market to become more revitalizing, invigorating, and stimulating. This consumer group was starting to enter a new age bracket that was accompanied by different needs and products that were more age-appropriate for them. The brand wanted to build a stronger connection to one of their most relevant target groups, the Millennials, born between the early '80s and mid-'90s, who have a large impact on the economy due to their spending habits. To put this into context, in the U.S. alone, according to Mintel's market research, Millennials are the largest generation and make up almost 25 percent of the entire population as of 2022, strongly redefining the consumer buying power in this market in addition to Gen Z.[6] At the time of this project at L'Oréal Germany, about 22 percent of the German population was made up of Millennials—just as powerful considering the smaller population count in Germany of around 84 million people.[7]

The brand intended to maximize the growth drivers under the umbrella of strength as its brand equity, which include building the love brand for stronger, healthier hair, driving penetration with on-top innovation. Additionally, Fructis had been suffering from an image disconnect, as the brand was inadvertently associated with a chemical focus. As a result, the new and more health-conscious Fructis aimed to move away from this image and respond to the more health-focused lifestyle of Millennials by offering a product that was silicone- and paraben-free while continuing to be vibrant. Introducing a brand-new formula accompanied by new packaging and marketing efforts, the brand focused on speaking the same Millennial language to better connect with their target audience. Across Germany, the hair care market was competing heavily with products that did not include silicone or paraben whereas in the U.S., the trend started a little later, focusing more on paraben-free products (and later sulfate-free) as a priority instead of both silicone- and paraben-free products. The product packaging, specifically the images used to represent the fruits and ingredients of the products, suggested that a more straightforward and honest identity with a less manufactured image would have a stronger appeal to the intended demographic. For Fructis, this was an opportunity to improve brand attributes like trust, closeness, and efficacy because without this, a love brand was out of question. Therefore, the focus became to build initiatives that triggered these brand attributes and turn a typically low-involvement category such as hair care into a love brand. After all, the so-called self-expressive brands are the brands consumers desire and love. With the key focus of how to rebrand the consumer mass market hair care brand Fructis, mainly geared towards the Millennial demographic, I developed recommendations for a successful relaunch as a love brand using insights from research, interviews, studies, and focus groups with influencers in the Millennial demographic that proved to be quite insightful.

Influencer marketing has emerged as a relevant part of many marketing plans and budgets over the years. Influencers who have higher-than-average reach are building millions of followers today because they're authentic. Consumers recognize that and bond with it. Social influencers have been able to grow huge followings via social media platforms, demonstrating they're able to engage audiences in attractive and innovative ways. Just like the luxury fashion brand DIOR Beauty did by launching the first campaign in the industry with South Korean global influencer and brand ambassador Jisoo over the messaging platform WhatsApp to empower conversations in a unique way, tapping into ways to personalize and innovate content.[8] So, what type of influencers do brands seek? Gaining a better understanding of marketing dynamics and segmenting product offerings based on consumers with different cultural needs, pushes them to rethink diversity across ethnicity, gender, and culture. Shouldn't brands who cater to a specific market of consumers be representative anyway? How else can a company target a group of people that it doesn't identify with? For that reason, it's important to develop plans that target multicultural audiences strategically.

L'Oréal is a great example of working with cultural influencers to reach an audience that's relevant to the company's multi-brand product offering. Although companies of this size have always been known to have traditional celebrity influencers to help promote brands and products, digital influencers convey a different value—one that can be more authentic and insightful. Influencers connect with customers in different and more direct ways where one can obtain feedback in real time—just how I did during my project. In the world of social influencing today, finding authentic and creative ways to elevate B2C cultural influencer marketing is fundamental. It's important to note, though, that a huge following doesn't necessarily equate to the right influencer for a brand. Through the cultural style of marketing, brands can reach diverse audiences in effective ways to engage a growing following and increase their bottom line.

The Garnier Fructis rebrand efforts resulted in a more vibrant Fructis with a shampoo proposition that highlights vitality and liveliness to hair as well as youth, pleasure, playfulness, and free self-expression. With new packaging, colors, fonts and product names like Aloe Hydra Bomb, Argan Silk & Shiny, Coco Water, Cucumber Fresh, or Wunder Butter (wonder butter in English), the brand made a move in the right direction to position itself to appeal more to the Millennial target audience, especially by speaking their Millennial language as reflected in the product names.[9] Fructis continues the brand journey of being trendsetting, inspiring, and unique in the German hair care market.

The shampoo category has "must-have" essentials, which explains factors that every shampoo brand has to deliver, though it's not enough to build strong differentiation. Basic category must-haves include product quality, trust, safety, naturalness (making it free from parabens, silicones, sulfates, and other preservatives), adaptability to different hairstyles, suitability, convenience, and good value for money. In addition to the basic features in the shampoo category, the consumer desires their hair to be in perfect health, bringing out natural beauty as a result. These needs are relevant in many European markets, but with country-specific nuances at times, local formula customization can be relevant. In Germany, for instance, women aspire to a more simple and friendly beauty and hair look. Product quality and brand reliability prove to be higher-ranking demands. German women are also keener on natural or mild sensorial experiences. Unique sensorial drivers as such offer the highest potential for differentiation and intimacy considering their strong connection to emotion. As you can see, it takes many elements to achieve the status of a love brand, including successful product packaging, naming, imagery, and communication that has to align with your target audience.

This example shows a good combination of how a brand can create brand desire and move toward intimacy across all stages in "The Eight Brand Love Stages" model, spanning from awareness to love, to reaching loyalty and advocacy after the new product hits the market.

Brand desire fuels growth

Being a force for motivation is more difficult for some brands than others, but you have to motivate people to buy the product after creating awareness. Still, there are things that people don't think about when they try to create a new product or service. Brands often underestimate how powerful brand desire is. This is a foundation you can build upon where you have to nurture this feeling throughout the life of your brand.

At the start of Blended Collective, we had people and new clients believe in us when nobody really knew who we were. This was simply because they believed in the mission and values that we had introduced through our communication efforts, allowing us to drive the distinctiveness of our brand as a new marketing and brand consulting firm and in an industry that was already saturated. We were living out our values and our community could see and feel it. Being accessible encouraged participation through various events we hosted, allowing us to create strong brand awareness in the early stages of brand building. We consider these clients our first movers and supporters; the people who took a chance on us and were willing to support us and build with us from day one. These are the people you want to build desire for first. Once we had created successful case studies, our clients turned into brand champions for our business, which made our work and marketing a lot more efficient as they advocated for our services and promoted our business through word of mouth. With so many marketing tools available nowadays, word of mouth is a powerful and inexpensive way to promote your brand. This is where quality over quantity matters. Isn't it better to have a few committed, passionate followers that love your brand instead of hundreds who don't engage at all? Earned credibility will always feel better—and last longer—than credibility that is purchased.

Whenever you put brand desire in the center of everything you do, you lay the foundation for your products and services to be pushed into the forefront. If you create brand desire for your customer and stay consistent with delivering great value over time, you have potential customers who will quickly move from the awareness and familiarity stage to a later stage to buy from you. And if they trust you and are happy, they will turn into a repeat, loyal customer. Remember, it's typically less expensive to retain your customers than to acquire new ones. And because it's difficult to create and sustain brand desire for everyone, it's best to start with your core target audience. To get people to desire your brand and fall in love with you, you have to understand their deepest and truest needs before you can activate and nurture brand desire.

Love Notes

1 **A brand is more than a logo**
Your brand makes up your visual identity and all consumer-brand interactions that gets people excited. If you get it right, it can serve you for the life of your brand as you connect with customers to share experiences.

2 **Your consumer is in the driver's seat**
Your brand is "owned" by your consumers as their perceptions shape the thoughts they have about your brand. They choose how to interact with brands and who to buy from based on the image they build about them in their mind.

3 **Understand your prospect's mind**
Start with the mind of your prospect to understand what experiences will activate their senses and make them desire your brand.

4 **Create brand desire for your core audience**
Focus on a small group first as it's difficult to create brand desire for everyone. Once you find ways to activate and nurture brand desire for growth, it's easier to expand your marketing efforts to reach larger groups of people over time.

03 Fostering self-identification and belonging

I gravitate toward brands and products that are simple yet unique. Brands who are original and different. I've always felt good when discovering something that not many people know about, whether it's a product, place, or a song. Most brands want to be embraced by the masses but the moment something becomes popular and part of mainstream culture, I personally lose interest. It doesn't feel special anymore.

The brands we use serve as a means of consumer self-expression and the "lifestyle we desire," which has an impact on consumer behavior and brand preferences as research shows.[1] The same research indicates that it's quite common for consumers to use brands who reflect who they are, or the identity they desire to communicate to the people around them.[2] Based on what people care about and the physical things they own, we make assumptions that they must be a certain way and try to put them in a box. Many ways exist to communicate who we are such as through the clothes we wear, our hairstyle, the music we listen to, the places we spend time at, or the places we travel to and explore.

When it comes to brands, consumers want to be aligned with a brand who stands for something more than what is being sold to them; they want brands with meaning that they can identify with and use to express their inner self and values—something they can use to show their lifestyle to the world without necessarily telling people who they are or trying to be. They want to be able to express their identity, ideally through their brands of choice. As their identity evolves, so does their decision to represent their values using different brands while moving through life. This helps people reinforce their status and how they want to be perceived by others.

Someone who buys a Gucci designer purse is not doing so purely for the functional benefits, or else they could carry a no-name purse. They are likely doing so because they want to be associated with luxury to some extent and signal their level of achievement to people around them. Or because they share the same values as the brand they choose. This is not to say that people don't buy such things simply because they enjoy the nicer things in life as a result of their hard work but typically, it seems to be more closely related to the image people want to paint or values they want to communicate—to themselves and others. People with certain affinities are attracted to specific brands. Yet, there are also people who make a statement about themselves by not choosing any brands at all. They're anti-brand.

The concept of self-expression, self-identification, or self-reflection is a foundational element for any brand who wants to develop an emotional connection with consumers that eventually leads to higher purchase intention, even if a brand checks the box for other drivers that can help toward the journey to brand love. Consistent, emotional connections with consumers are at the heart of what modern brands do. "The Eight Brand Love Stages" indicate that self-identification begins closer to the likeness stage. For a consumer to identify with a brand, there needs to be some level of connection and likeness. Or sometimes the sense of self a brand encourages is what inspires consumers to gravitate toward it.

How Huda Beauty encourages a sense of self

The billion-dollar cosmetics empire brand Huda Beauty by Iraqi-American Huda Kattan gained popularity through her beauty blog in 2010. Since the launch of her brand in 2013, the brand has become a recognizable beauty brand across the globe with products that span from face, eyes, lips, cheek, to body, and with an audience that doesn't seem to stop growing. Huda Beauty seems to promote the idea of self-expression, supported by the brand's marketing campaigns that empower their target audience to get in touch with their inner beauty. You can tell the community means a lot to the brand considering the way they choose to engage with their millions of followers across their social media platforms. Instagram alone boasts 52 million followers as of early 2023.[3] The platforms showcase different launches and reasons behind their many actions, so that it resonates with consumers well but also builds trust over time.

Huda seems to understand what her customers are looking for, and she clearly delivers on this in creative and innovative ways. But most importantly to her, the products she sells to consumers empower people to "express who they want to be no matter who they are or where they are from."[4] After all, beauty is in the eye of the beholder. Much of the core of the brand is focused on the customer being able to not only identify themselves with beauty through the brand but to express themselves confidently and as they are, disrupting the idea of beauty others often lean on that focuses on perception. This is likely one of the reasons that the brand's following is so loyal, in addition to taking inspiration from customers who share their feedback and insights on the brand's social media channels, which then inspires product development ideas. This is also one of the many brand drivers that contributes to the journey of brand love Huda Beauty appears to check off—the brand's ability to innovate through constant product development to fill a gap in the beauty marketplace, with products becoming instant best-sellers across the globe. Or the ability to build a strong community and bond with people, also with user-generated content.

Let's look at Huda's second brand launch, WISHFUL, which, according to the brand, was created because of consumer insights over the years for a more simple and gentle skincare routine, marketed as "clean & intentional."[5] To reflect the natural approach of the products, the brand shared at launch that it would be a no Photoshop or retouching brand, encouraging people to cultivate their most natural side of who they are.[6] I appreciate brands who join the "no retouching movement" in an effort to promote natural and authentic beauty by normalizing such looks. It feels refreshing for a change to see someone who looks like you without makeup. I believe that any brand who makes it possible to not have to keep up with unrealistic beauty standards and deal with social pressure to look a certain way, will be able to make strong changes in the beauty industry. I've seen more brands join this movement in recent years, which I applaud, especially considering social media platforms that are known to exaggerate beauty looks that both adults and teenagers feel like they have to match to "fit in." Sometimes I even catch myself scrolling through my social media feed and getting stuck on pages with women portraying such perfect looks from head to toe. At the same time though, I'm pretty good and disciplined about reminding myself that this is not who I am (or want to be) and then snapping out of such social media illusions quickly. Part of this I contribute to being a marketer and simply being aware of how this social media game works.

Among all loved brands across industries, beauty and fashion brands appear to be the most tapped into what their customers are looking for. They rely on things like the passion of their customers, their trust (clean skincare!), and satisfaction.

Beauty industry as inspiration

Take, for instance, Dove's Self-Esteem Project, where every young person is encouraged to reach their full potential[7] and enter a world that is removed from toxic beauty standards.[8] Dove's website is full of topics and open conversations about helping young people overcome body image issues, so that they can build positive body confidence and self-esteem.[9] Free resources span from advice for parents and mentors on raising a confident child, body confidence workshops that teachers and educators can organize, to activities and topic discussions for young leaders to reach young people.[10] Articles are available across multiple topics that can be tailored based on the appropriate age group.[11] Within the resources they've made available online is a guide called "Help your child develop a positive body image."[12] It covers conversations about self-image, fashion, and cosmetic surgery.[13] Providing a resource for parents and children to share their stories and have these important conversations is crucial, as children navigate the daily pressures of social media telling them what they should look like to "fit in." Dove, who we know and recognize as a brand who champions body positivity and inclusivity, does this right. They offer ways for customers to not only identify with the products but also to connect deeply with the brand through their brand's identity. Content that prompts conversations or audience engagement allows customers to foster their self-identification and utilize brands they can see themselves in.

Whether you're leading a brand in the beauty industry or not, you should always look at other industries for inspiration. To be innovative and different in your brand approach, what can you find in a different industry that can be applied to your brand?

I was in a client meeting once where we discussed how we could drum up the number of members in an organization. Instead of encouraging a few members to recruit 10 members during a dedicated period of time, what if we encouraged every member to recruit only one member? In an organization with thousands of members, this goes a long way. It also seems more doable overall. The inspiration for this came from a Sainsbury's case study I had come across a few months prior. Sainsbury's is a supermarket chain in the U.K. that encouraged every customer to spend an extra £ 1.14 whenever they shopped.[14] Using multimedia outlets to reach shoppers and sharing meal ideas that would inspire them to try and buy new products helped the supermarket chain raise their bottom line by over £550 million over a two-year period.[15]

If done right, your brand can strive to become a love brand, too.

The beauty industry is a unique space you can learn a lot from whether it's the customization aspect of products, diversifying the industry, or embracing natural beauty that mirrors the self or conveys values of authenticity. In Part Two of the book where I talk about emotional drivers, I will go into more detail about other brand examples and methods for how you can implement some of these efforts I mentioned. Throughout the book, I weave in brand examples to portray how many of these concepts apply in a global context. To set the foundation for this, let's move on to the importance of why cultural representation matters for brands who want to be successful with their marketing.

Cultural representation matters: what people see when they see themselves

Sometimes brands think it's enough to translate their marketing content into their target audience's language like Spanish or Arabic to sell their brand, build a connection, and support multilingual customers, so they can feel a sense of representation. Working in the multicultural marketing space, this is almost never the right answer. According to government census data, 50 percent of the U.S. population alone is going to be multicultural by 2044.[16] This means that every other person will be of multicultural descent, mainly coming from one of three major cultural groups that are typically referenced in the marketing industry: Black, Asian American, and Hispanic or Latino. With such a diverse consumer base that continues to grow, the buying power of these three groups is increasing tremendously and will continue to increase, so brands should be mindful as to how to market to these groups. When you cater to multicultural consumer groups with different attitudes and consumer behavior, these are likely not the result only of their cultural backgrounds; they come with different sets of factors that affect every step throughout the consumer-brand journey, whether it's around their education, upbringing, gender, thoughts, or experiences. People are intersectional, and you can't just take one element of their cultural heritage or identity and apply it to your marketing strategy.

To reach them effectively, it takes a lot more to appeal to your target audience, especially when they're representative of a specific cultural group. The truth is, within that group, it's a far fetch to claim they're all the same. What about subgroups of different races, ethnic and identity groups? Consumers have several needs, and we can't segment them based on demographics solely but rather on these needs. So, how do you get it right? Culture matters. Representation matters—in all regards. The right representation and quality are what matters; what we need more of is representative content and marketing that is non-stereotypical.

When you're watching a TV show, for example, different cultures should be shown in various settings. We're conditioned to think about certain cultures based on what we see growing up and hence make associations with what we see for ourselves. For instance, my friend's three-year-old daughter Alyse typically associates any meal that is cooked at home with her father as she knows he's the one who cooks. Gone are the days when mom was thought of as the main person to stand in the kitchen and put food on the table. In my Middle Eastern culture, women traditionally stayed home, cooked, and looked after the kids, which is the picture that was displayed heavily across multimedia channels, especially on TV, for decades. But putting Middle Eastern women into a more realistic context, they are now portrayed as working mothers, business owners, and wives, known to be fierce and independent.

When we think about Middle Eastern and North African (MENA) representation, however, the biggest gap in the U.S. is that we're not able to identify our race and ethnicity properly when it comes to completing the U.S. Census every 10 years to map out the population and demographics. Based on this, random forms we fill out in our everyday lives such as for jobs, online surveys, or at the doctor's office, are oftentimes mirrored like the Census and therefore, don't include a selection for MENA. Instead, the classification is "white."

Personally, I don't feel like this is the best reflection of my identity. Though I was born and raised in Germany, my parents are Chaldean, a Christian minority group from Iraq. Having to check the "white" category, which clusters cultures such as German, Italian, and Lebanese into one and the same group, doesn't feel like an honest expression or representation of my community. And, when I was growing up, I wasn't sure where I belonged culturally. In Germany, to this day, people identify me as a "foreigner" as my parents don't have "German blood." Whenever I visit any country in the Middle East, I'm considered German or European because I didn't grow up or live in the Middle East. And finally, in the U.S., some people see me as German, Middle Eastern, or sometimes both—go figure. Whew, and you wonder how someone can be culturally confused.

At home, my sister and I experienced a traditional, Middle Eastern upbringing with our parents. Outside of the house, we assimilated and adapted our cultural identities to mix with our German and European friends. What seemed like a good balance was confusing to a child. As children, we wanted to fit in (even if my dad still jokes that I always had to be different and stand out). After coming to the U.S., it added a third layer of culture to my life that, again, wasn't easy to adapt to but was rewarding in hindsight. This has taught me a valuable lesson that it's not ideal to cluster customers into the same bucket due to being part of the "same" culture. The simplest way to compare this is to look at me growing up in Germany to Chaldean parents and look at Chaldeans who grew up in the U.S. We are different on so many levels culturally because I had other environmental and social influences that affected my upbringing, behavior, and thoughts. It's not better or worse, just different. The culture we grow up in has an impact on how we operate and exist in the world. I'm thankful for my multicultural upbringing and being able to experience, live, and identify with three cultures that span three continents day-to-day, impacting the way I navigate business and cultures constantly.

As brands create and plan their marketing to reach and engage people like myself, they need to understand the layers of who we are, even within the same cultures. Culture impacts the way we see the world. This ultimately affects consumer behavior and purchase decisions.

The multicultural consumer path

According to Nielsen, one of the multicultural groups in the market, Asian Americans, is the fastest-growing group of Americans and includes subgroups like people who are East Asian, South and Southeast Asian, or Asian Pacific Islander.[17] They continue to be of great influence when it comes to trends, such as Asian food being part of people's diet, the K-pop culture, creating content, and a buying power that has tripled between the '90s and 2021 and doesn't see an end in sight.[18] Yet, Asians feel like there is not enough representation of them on TV and when there is, the portrayal of them is inaccurate.[19] I can understand how this can be the case considering the many countries Asian Americans come from. It is not only important to create content that is sensitive to their values and who they are but also to communicate in a way that proves relevant to them.

To set the bar for representation of Black audiences, representation of the community remains important, too. According to Nielsen, this consumer group pays attention to the stories that are being told and how they are showing up across various genres in the same way they're paying attention to who is sitting in company boardrooms, which is where a lot of the decision-making filters from the top to the bottom.[20] With a Black buying power to reach $1.8 trillion in 2024,[21] Black consumers are usually more likely to consume content that is representative of them as well as buy brands who focus their marketing and advertising efforts around representative content.[22] In times where consumers are much more aware of the effort brands make to reach and engage them, it only makes sense to create the right content based on the audience you want to reach. If a consumer can see themselves in a brand, isn't it safe to say they feel some type of connection from the start? Disregard whether they end up buying or not. From the get-go, you're already closer to making them feel seen and valued.

According to Nielsen, Hispanic or Latino audiences, the largest multicultural group among all three of them, make up about 20 percent of the U.S. population at the time of writing.[23] Additional insight from Nielsen recognizes that it is important to understand that many in this group belong to two or more races, so when brands understand this intersectionality, they can start to integrate an inclusive narrative into ad creative, media content, and other consumer engagement efforts.[24] All in all, brands should focus on engaging various multicultural markets authentically, so that everyone feels included.

Connect with your audience by meeting them where they are

When I moved back to Germany in my 20s, I was browsing the grocery store to discover the brands and products across categories that I had missed out on throughout the years. True Fruits, a German smoothie company beloved by many European markets, captured my attention right away. Their packaging featured statements such as, "You don't suck as much," "Bullshit," or "Bayern" to represent the professional soccer team in Germany, focused on a healthy lifestyle-oriented product.[25] Looking at their Instagram page while writing this, I see a cherry blossom smoothie that features Japanese characters, or others that are co-branded with popular German brands in the market and across industries such as the Em-eukal cherry flavor herbal drop with the little kid on the red package.[26] Years after discovering the brand, I'm still intrigued.

What adds another cool factor is that you can recycle their bottles, but also repurpose them in other ways. The brand showcases ingenious ways to recycle these bottles as a soap dispenser, a spray bottle, sugar holder, or a pepper mill. These various bottle attachments or covers are available on the brand's website,[27] adding a sustainable component to the brand's core, which has proven to have a huge impact on bringing a consumer closer to a brand. Its entire line of communication sounds exactly like the way the Millennial and Gen Z demographic speaks—it's like they're friends and the brand knows what they want to hear to capture their attention. It's different and makes people feel as though they are part of the conversation. It isn't communication directed *at* us but, rather, *with* us as if the brand knows exactly who we are.

True Fruits understands the consumer mindset and leverages its space by speaking the same language as its audience both online and offline. Whether you see it on the shelves at the supermarket or scroll through the Instagram page on your phone, the experience is seamless and smooth; it's consistent across the board. When working with clients, I make sure to emphasize the importance of creating consistency across all channels as it relates to branding and marketing.

The food and beverage industry, besides beauty and fashion, is notorious for fostering ways of self-identification, reflection, or expression for consumers. One of Lindt's campaigns had me at *HELLO*, as it was making efforts to market a brand who caters to their coveted Millennial audience through a digital-focused launch, including social platforms. The chocolate bars, along with their creative and eye-catching marketing, have contributed to a successful presence of

Lindt's brand *HELLO* to reach a previously untapped youth cohort in the premium chocolate category.[28] To do so, the brand engages customers by focusing on promotional campaigns that correlate to the lifestyle of Millennials using the hashtag #LindtHELLO.[29] This audience enjoys music and spending time with friends and family, especially in the summertime. Accordingly, Lindt launched seasonal giveaways, some connected to music.[30] The brand established a very casual way of communicating to Millennials using pronouns and the claim "*Nice to sweet you.*" It's a simple yet thoughtful way of connecting with playful language and individuality, which is also reflected in the different color variations of chocolate offerings, ingredients, and unusual flavors, giving each a personality of its own.[31] Each chocolate bar is given a voice on the vibrant packaging with funny and attention-grabbing introductions, talking to consumers directly with attractive taglines. It's an authentic and funny way to engage with an audience in an effort to win their attention.

The idea of giving chocolate a character can be seen with Ferrero's Kinder Chocolate, too, where the product ingredients are shown as Mr. Chocolate and Ms. Milk. Aspects like the heart-shaped images and love mentions across their product packaging and boxes allow it to be interpreted as an effort to establish a love brand among Millennials.

When I was living in Germany in 2015 and 2016, this brand was heavily advertised across all customer touchpoints at the point of sale as well as online to the point where even their website domain was lovebrands.com. Younger demographic groups are particular about how they communicate with each other. If you want to have a chance of reaching them, bridge the communication gap and speak like them. When you don't speak the same language, customers can feel the disconnect and tune out, pushing them to look for other brands who appeal to them more and show that they "get them."

Who do you want to be (with)?

As this is a book about brand love, I would be doing you a disservice if I didn't dive into brands who market love and relationships. Dating apps like Bumble, Hinge, or Tinder might be like other dating apps that exist but what makes them stand out is the swipe-based technology that makes you swipe right if you like the person or left if you dislike them. Finding love online through dating apps has been instrumental in people connecting, forging meaningful relationships, or even getting married as stigmas around online dating seem to be less and less. And if it's not a fit on either end and you keep swiping and swiping without finding "the one," you either end up getting "ghosted" or simply deleting the app.

As individuals, we spend our entire lives creating and developing our unique personal brand and image—even when we're not aware of it. The personal brand we create is as unique as we are as individuals. No two human beings are the same. Just like the 2022 British Airways campaign confirms. The efforts aim to restore brand love with the idea that every individual is unique. By launching 500 unique ads, each one is supposed to represent a unique reason why people fly.[32] At the end of the day, the way we conduct ourselves, our beliefs and values, the story or message we share, and the image we project, are all pieces that contribute to our personal brand that makes us unique.

Your online dating profile reflects who you think you are or, in some cases, who you want to be. I like to compare it to the elevator pitch we are taught to practice as entrepreneurs. In 30–60 seconds, you need to communicate the core of what you're all about without diving deep into your history or background. You basically focus on the most important aspects you want people to know about you. What matters and why should anyone care?

We position ourselves on these apps to display the best and most attractive version of ourselves, and it's quite similar to the way many of us promote our brands. We want an interaction to indicate who we are, what we're all about, and why we matter. So, what's your value proposition and why should anyone swipe right on you instead of anyone else? As it relates to the world of brands and consumerism, why should anyone buy your brand instead of a competitor's?

In the world of online dating, people are sometimes looked at as a commodity as opposed to a real person. It can feel like you're relentlessly shopping and hunting for another human. Like you're browsing through a vintage store to find this one unique piece of clothing, but in the end, you're left disappointed as you realize nothing stands out. Everything is the same; nothing fits you. On dating apps, you have to scroll through thousands of profiles while you ask yourself questions like: Does this person look trustworthy? Transparent? Could they be a potential stalker? You have to differentiate yourself as your own personal brand with your attributes. You are presenting the version that describes you best and makes you most appealing to someone you've never met, to stand out in a crowded marketplace where people are overwhelmed with choices, the same way as when you're standing in the chips or cereal aisle at the grocery store.

While each of these online dating apps promotes a similar goal—for users to find someone to date—the essence of each app goes much deeper. Whereas Bumble is viewed as a more mature app and woman-friendly, putting the woman in charge of the dating process (though you can also use the app to find friends or business contacts), Tinder is known as an app that encourages you to keep dating and use the app with no end in sight. Hinge, on the other hand, was "designed to be deleted." You find what you're looking for and you delete your profile. Yup, it's that simple. The value proposition of each dating app is quite different, but the parallels between online dating and marketing remain comparable in that they both demand trust and a genuine sense of belonging to be successful.

Cultivate a sense of belonging and community

Belonging elicits overall positive sentiment as it describes a human emotion where we feel a sense of acceptance and connectedness to other groups and communities. It's the feeling that you're a part of something and that you're not alone. You feel welcome. You feel safe. You feel connected. All of this comes with a feeling of belonging. The job of marketing is to understand people and their needs to effectively cater to them. While marketing in the traditional sense consisted of building brands and products to market them to potential customers and make a sale after the fact, this is certainly no longer the case. You can't build a brand and expect people to show up and buy. It just doesn't work like this anymore. Companies today are more deliberate with the brands they build. And in some cases, they make a conscious decision to activate their brands by placing their community in the center of it.

Streetwear brands who convey a cool style and represent good vibes are known to grow communities. The game-changing industry includes many of them. One of my favorites is the woman-owned and operated sport lifestyle brand Melody Ehsani (ME.), whom I've been following since her early days. Melody opened a women's boutique on Fairfax in Los Angeles with streetwear brands like Supreme and Diamond on the same block.

The ME. brand started online, just what the streetwear community is known for. Making and selling footwear and jewelry out of her car caught the attention of high-profile entertainers in the music industry and beyond. I remember in the early days of the brand, when her jewelry designs were worn by celebrities like Alicia Keys and graced album covers of artists like Erykah Badu, showing support of the young designer brand at the time. With a storefront that followed a few years later, the brand quickly grew into what it seems it was meant to be all along—an activation space to drive community at the core. The store is not your traditional lifestyle store you visit to shop and leave. ME. hosts events, including a previous speaker series to discuss issues that revolve around culture, social justice, design, and sport.

Clothing tags on one of my hoodies seem to reinforce the community brand pillar to let customers know they matter and are valued by using phrases such as, "I'm so happy you exist." Or the candle in my bathroom that I bought during my time in Los Angeles that reads:

> This candle was made with love, with the intention to bring love into your space. Love is the only thing that makes us remember who we truly are. What do you love the most? Who do you love to be with? There is information & memory in those situations—that's why love is so important. The answer is always love.[33]

I also can't forget about the ME. and Reebok partnership to design the iconic Allen Iverson sneaker *The Question*. I made sure to grab a pair before they sold out and I would find myself on StockX, the online marketplace for all things streetwear. The message supports a generation who can "hold her own," so much so that this is printed on the tongue of the sneaker. Features such as Iverson's tattoos that can be swapped and attached to the back of the shoe with a Velcro patch while the interior features his cornrows, are all designed to embody the core of the Allen Iverson brand. This is such a well-thought-out, creative, meaningful design and message that I still appreciate as I'm staring at the shoe while writing this.

Over the years, brands have grown to be more vocal to have a voice in the community on issues that matter, which they want to attach themselves to—just like ME. and The Hundreds. The Hundreds is another streetwear brand who focuses on community. Founded by Bobby Kim and Ben Shenassafar in 2003, The Hundreds "houses a classic California streetwear brand and media platform dedicated to global street culture."[34] They pride themselves on providing their own perspective on streetwear while telling the story of the underdog.[35] The Hundreds emphasizes people over product while placing a high importance on personal expression.[36] With this belief, this brand, too, occupies a unique position in the marketplace to provide clothing for people to express themselves and share their stories across communities on a global scale.

I've seen other brands like Lululemon and Tory Burch activate their brands around community with a focus on in-store community events. Or celebrity brands like the Kardashians who built a community with SKIMS and Good American around their size-inclusive brands who have grown into multiple categories. When brands do what these have done, they root themselves in a community. This helps brands keep the word of mouth going and the support strong. To build a strong community, these are the following thoughts I encourage when working with brands:

1. Understand why your brand exists—what is your "why"? Your purpose?
2. Pinpoint the core values you represent.
3. Listen to your target audience you want to reach to learn what they value.
4. Identify your shared purpose, values, and what makes you different in a competitive space.

5 Speak your audience's language and meet them where they are.
6 Connect and share stories.
7 Focus on building, growing, and nurturing your community.

Brand value is cultivated through community. Building a community takes work and a lot of dedication over long periods of time, so it's important to be intentional about how to cultivate it. Making community a part of your marketing strategy offers new opportunities as you develop and build relationships that take trust and time to flourish. Sometimes negative and honest feedback might make you feel like you're taking a step back, but this is also part of community-building, so that you can authentically keep improving your skillset to grow your community past clicks and conversions. As humans, we have a need for connection and a desire to be a part of something. When we recognize that we can bond with others over topics and share interests on our customer journey, the brands who put their customers first make space for them to connect in this special way. The intrinsic understanding results in people connecting deeply on a social and emotional level to come together through these shared moments. They want to support a brand they're passionate about, especially when they're encouraged to be themselves.

Love Notes

1 **Self-identification is a foundational element**
The idea of self-identification, expression, or reflection constitutes a major concept of brand love. Think of ways customers can connect with you in a way where you mirror their values to them with the help of your brand.

2 **Culture matters**
Culture has an impact on how we see the world. It's important to understand not all customers in one and the same culture can be clustered into the same customer group. Spend time to learn and understand their key cultural differences as it affects their decision-making process and choice of brand.

3 **Meet your customers where they are**
Speak like them. Remember that meeting your customers where they are to make them feel like they belong can be a tremendous way to boost your brand affinity.

4 **Center your brand around community**
Let there be community. Building a community can be challenging but over time you will attract people who want to bond with you and others where they can share values and purpose. When people are inspired, they come together to support in strong ways. We all want to be a part of something bigger that empowers and leaves us better.

PART TWO
Emotional drivers

Living brand authenticity

04

When you're an authentic brand, it's all about being genuine and real. You're straightforward and honest about your mission and values—you walk the talk. Your customers don't have to think twice about whether you can be trusted or not. Still, authenticity is a word that is overused in marketing and labeled as one of the busiest buzzwords (probably besides diversity and purpose).

Everyone wants to be authentic and show up as their true self or "whole self" at work too, but what does that really mean? Is it being able to live out what we think and say? As the cultural landscape continues to evolve, we see more and more consumers communicating a desire to express who they are and who they want to be on a personal level without having to fear not being accepted in the workplace. You can hear and read it everywhere: in webinars, articles, reports, and all throughout social platforms. And then you have brands like Peloton who make it part of their mission by "empowering people to be the best version of themselves, anywhere, anytime."[1] Over time, this concept of authenticity has spilled into the business world where consumers, especially Gen Z, search for brands who "keep it real" and present themselves to the public as their true self.

As a brand, you have to tap into the core of who you are as this is part of the reason why customers connect with you. In the pursuit of brand authenticity, brands should be rooted in their values and encompass brand attributes like honesty, reliability, transparency, trustworthiness, and truth. Now, what does authenticity mean to your brand? How can you create and live it in a way that resonates with your customers in an authentic way?

Don't say it, live it

Building an authentic brand can be difficult but being reliable, trustworthy, true, honest, and transparent is an effective way to connect with your customers who make it clear that they want more from the brands they support. In fact, it's the only way if you want to continue to climb the ladder in "The Eight Brand Loves Stages" to reach brand love by becoming a trustworthy and beloved brand. And guess what? Doing it wrong is almost worse than not doing it at all, so brands have to convince people that they really mean what they say; that they're authentic. Don't you expect the same in your personal life? When someone's actions don't align with their words, what does this reveal about their attitudes and beliefs? When this happens, people recognize it as a red flag and are quick to label them as unreliable and not trustworthy.

When I was being interviewed for the Branch Out Podcast by Connection Builders to talk about "Taking Control of Your Personal Brand," the podcast host made a good point, saying, "I don't know many people or brands who say, 'Well, I want to be inauthentic.' But many people will say, 'Well, authentic is something I want to be.'"[2] I chuckled when I heard this because it's true. No brand makes a statement saying they don't care about being authentic, but actions speak louder than words. Brands can talk a good talk all day long but if they don't put their money where their mouth is, it's just lip service—and at the end of the day, that's meaningless. Consumers are intuitive and it's easy to tell which brands care about it because when they're intentional, they prioritize it as a driving value. In a nutshell, brand authenticity can't be engineered.

During times of uncertainty or crisis, brands can impact the perceptions customers hold of their brand by choosing to communicate in a genuine way that aligns with their brand identity and core values.[3] Whenever brands try too hard to be authentic without a genuine effort, it can seem like a marketing gimmick that customers quickly spot. As a result, they lose trust and respect for the brand, causing more harm than good in the long run.

In a 2020 white paper on "Brand Authenticity" by Escalent, a data analytics and advisory firm that has helped clients navigate disruption by understanding human and market behaviors since the '70s, research results were shared from interviewing a national sample of 1,000 consumers aged 18 and older, as well as examining thousands of brand ratings across various industries.[4] By mapping out five elements of what it means to be an authentic brand, authenticity was found to be multidimensional beyond what I shared.[5] The five elements were found to be thoughtful, transparent, reliable, committed, and socially aware.[6] Together they create a single index that reflects consumers' perception, simplifies competitive benchmarking, and allows for ways to better understand how brand authenticity can be improved.[7] The brands who score highly in this category are the ones who know who they are and whose values are intrinsic to what they do and how they do it. Understanding how this relates to consumer needs is important. One of the top performers is the U.S. grocery chain Trader Joe's, who scored highly across all five categories in the study, especially for transparency.[8]

How Trader Joe's acts authentically with its values

The grocery store is known as the chain that eliminates the middleman, which can be attributed as part of its success. It's just you and Trader Joe's. During the COVID-19 pandemic, their response was considered sincere according to consumers who, as a result, viewed the brand more positively, although the brand experienced some backlash for their culturally insensitive branding and packaging of international foods.[9] In any case, the brand states what it stands for and is thoughtful and transparent when it comes to addressing this packaging issue.[10] Personally, I think Trader Joe's appreciates cultures and is fun after all. They seem to successfully bridge the cultural gap to introduce popular items that many customers wouldn't be exposed to or try otherwise, such as the gluten-free Middle Eastern falafel mix or the Greek spanakopita, an authentic spinach and cheese pie. Trader Joe's is a grocery store that customers are proud to be associated with and will let others know it's their place to shop, to the point that a customer and 95.7 West Michigan radio host wrote a letter declaring her love for the brand, starting it off with, "this is not an endorsement. It's simply a letter professing my love to the greatest grocery retailer":

> Dear TJ,
>
> First off, thank you for existing. Grocery shopping is one of the most vexing tasks of adulting. But you... you make the experience enjoyable thanks to your variety of unique offerings.
>
> Sure, you may not be as big as some of the other guys in the area, but I've never met anyone like you. I know what to expect when I walk in but at the same time, I get surprises along the way. You add a twist to the mundane foods and offer a range of eccentricity that radiates from one aisle to the next.
>
> TJ's your name but diversity is your game. From Mexican to Mediterranean munchies, Indian and Cuban cravings, to the Asian and Italian favorites. You make my stomach and my heart equally happy.
>
> Whether it's as French toast or the bread for my gourmet grilled cheeses, your brioche toast is a simple pleasure of mine. Your chili-spiced dried mangoes serve as a satisfying sweet and spicy snack that I don't feel bad about afterwards. Don't get me started on your Greek yogurt chunky guacamole. Oh my gosh, I can easily eat half the container. Your turkey corn dogs make a great quick and delicious meal when I don't feel like cooking. Your multiple types of pre-made salads and frozen meals are what hits the spot when I'm at work. The array of sauces and seasoning blends tantalize all my tastebuds. And that addicting Sparkling French Lemonade of yours quenches my thirst.
>
> TJ, I could go on and on about everything that I admire and love about you but there just isn't enough time. So just know that you will always be #1. Until next time.
>
> Yours truly,
> Christine[11]

Trader Joe's is a popular choice among customers; they seem to simply love it. Part of the reason appears to be rooted in the brand's consistency as well as the surprise element that's embedded in the consumer-brand experience, but also the continued product innovation customers enjoy as conveyed in this love letter. Let's not forget the engaged and enthusiastic staff. I feel the warmth of the conversation every time I shop there, especially when I get to end the experience with one of their kind cashiers. These individuals always make a point to ask about my day and weekend plans, and I always leave with a few items I didn't know I needed before I saw them on display.

Employees who are nice and friendly should be a standard everywhere you shop, but it seems as though Trader Joe's wins in this category consistently. Creating this employee culture could be intentional and part of the employee training. If it is, it certainly helps add elements of authenticity to the brand. The brand also has a local neighborhood vibe while offering unique products that are globally sourced with what at present seems to be a multicultural touch. The unique product packaging and descriptions, supported by adjectives that are different and part of the brand language, make you feel like you're getting a special product and high value with every purchase. Even as a marketer, I'm still intrigued by the words they use on the packaging.

It seems like customers want the perception of choice when in reality, all it takes is a smooth shopping experience for even someone like the radio host who wrote the letter to fall in love with a store like Trader Joe's. Having options is good, but according to a research study, too many choices are overwhelming and confusing for consumers.[12] For me, when having to decide between too many choices, it usually results in no decision at all. After a long day at work and experiencing so-called *decision fatigue*, I typically look forward to heading to the grocery store to shop. My friends make fun of how much I enjoy grocery shopping, but I love exploring different products, looking at the branding and marketing, and grabbing unique items that are difficult to find anywhere else. I especially feel this way when I travel to new places abroad where I always make time to visit local supermarkets to discover new cultural products, but also some that have been locally adapted with different packaging, imagery, descriptions, and of course, new ingredients in some cases. What I find interesting at Trader Joe's is the issue of scarcity for certain products that are discontinued regularly only for new ones to be introduced. I've experienced it one too many times. Trader Joe's is a loved brand who is difficult to copy. Yet, even with their many competitive advantages, it's not considered a one-stop shop.

Per Escalent's suggestions, using customer feedback to make decisions about their products and taking a stance about their brand packaging and communicating in a transparent way adds thoughtfulness.[13] To be viewed as even more authentic, another suggestion is made that the brand could consider bringing their customers into the conversation and allow them to be part of the product naming process for different food categories,[14] especially as it relates to different cultural products where particular cultural (sub)groups could contribute. Other brands in the food category such as HARIBO in the German market, which I talk about in this book, and Lay's chips in the U.S. with their *Do Us a Flavor* campaign,[15] encourage their customers to help them select new product flavors that are then released on store shelves for purchase. As long as customers are included as part of the process to support brands and products they can believe in, they will show support and loyalty.

Being honest and transparent

I mentioned Huda Beauty in Chapter 3 regarding helping customers achieve their sense of self through the brand, but when it comes to brand drivers like honesty and transparency, the brand continues to lead. When a social media comment about the product development process of creating the first mascara arose, founder Huda Kattan took to Instagram to address the follower's curiosity in all detail and transparency.[16] She describes that a follower made a statement that clinical trials were not allowed for mascaras, questioning the brand's explanation of why the product development process had taken such a long time. Posting a video on her Instagram platform, Huda clarifies the process of creating a mascara that was five years in the making, including pigmentation, formulation, brush, and testing, with a year spent on packaging as part of the product development process.[17] Huda confirms that, in fact, any product development process takes two years at the very minimum from ideation to execution in the beauty industry.[18] She goes on to say that, due to selling in so many markets, the brand has to go through a compliance process that backs up the claims it makes, such as the mascara being waterproof or lasting 48 hours, as an example.[19]

Addressing the follower's comment with her team members, who have worked for global brands in the industry, Huda continues that the social media statement was indeed proven wrong.[20] While a brand can choose to make informal statements that don't always have to be backed up by a lab, she says other statements such as claims about the volume and density of the mascara do have to be backed up by the clinical side.[21] I remember such insights from the time I was working in the beauty industry and how testing like this could be required depending on the brand, ingredients, and other factors. It doesn't matter if it's hair care, skincare, or makeup. To continue to drive the values of authenticity in the product marketing campaign to launch the mascara, Huda insisted on using models with basic, normal lashes. She refused to use models with beautiful lashes or photoshop them unlike other beauty standards in the industry.[22]

In this nearly ten-minute video, you can sense Huda's passion not only for her small beauty brand that is available in international and major retail, but also her passion to share the process through brand values such as honesty and transparency by letting people into the product development process with great detail. Where brands don't even bother to respond or issue a generic statement on their social media page to clear the air, Huda Beauty seems to go above and beyond the average beauty brand. With such a customer-centric approach, the brand shows a strong level of caring in the right way and at the right time, even when social media followers sometimes choose to not express much love online. According to Talkwalker, when brands find ways to mitigate the negative sentiment around them regardless of how big or small, they are one step closer to becoming a loved brand.[23] And the examples are no different in the food industry.

When KFC responded to the U.K. chicken shortage issue of 2018, the KFC name suddenly turned into a "FCK, we're sorry" campaign by the brand.[24] How can a fast-food chain known for fried chicken run out of chicken? Good question. The issue was the chicken supplier: it pushed hundreds of stores to close because of a lack of supply.[25] The situation wasn't the best, but it happened and there was no way to hide the fact that there was no chicken, so closing many stores certainly required some sort of explanation to customers. An ad that appeared in the *Metro* and *The Sun* newspapers read, "A chicken restaurant without any chicken. It's not ideal. Huge apologies to our customers, especially those who traveled out of their way to find we were closed. And endless thanks to our KFC team members and our franchise partners for working tirelessly to improve the situation. It's been a hell of a week, but we're making progress, and every day more and more fresh chicken is being delivered to our restaurants. Thank you for bearing with us."[26] Turning an issue into a situation many can laugh about shows a brand is human and is allowed to mess up, too. KFC dealt with this issue instantly and genuinely.

And why not add humor to the situation while you're at it? This is exactly what resonates with people when you're honest and transparent about the situation at hand and include them to be part of the journey that sometimes has a bumpy path. Like anything in life, it can be uncomfortable and rough but it's in uncomfortable moments like this where you grow. Anything you choose to do should reinforce the existing narrative. Customers understand because brands are like humans—we all make mistakes.

Controversial marketing efforts are a useful way to capture the attention of your audiences. Being controversial and pushy in their marketing seems to be part of Burger King's ad and media strategy and this campaign was no different under Fernando Machado, Chief Marketing Officer at the time for the restaurant group that includes Burger King, Popeyes, and Tim Hortons. Does anyone else remember Burger King's "The Moldy Whopper" campaign from 2020? Introduced in Sweden by agencies INGO, DAVID Miami, and Publicis,[27] the moldy whopper wasn't a new menu item; it seems to have been a strategic marketing approach to inform individuals that the iconic Whopper was removing artificial preservatives.[28] While it makes me question whether all these preservatives were part of the recipe until then, there's still something nice about seeing an open and honest change in this space. Something that wasn't portrayed as flawless in ads, as we're used to seeing. Some may have considered it positive while others viewed the ad as dramatic, negative, or even gross to look at—a burger with mold doesn't have much appeal to it.[29] I can understand why some would consider it as such but on the other hand, it's such a confident, powerful statement for such an iconic burger in the fast-food industry. Regardless, in moments like this, transparency can drive trust.

Keep it real

Other brands choose a more straightforward approach to marketing. Consider RXBAR. Their ingredients label reads: "Three egg whites. Six almonds. Four cashews. Two dates. No B.S."[30] These are the five ingredients listed on an RXBAR protein bar displayed in bold lettering to convey one of the brand pillars focused around selling only real ingredients, which is also strategically communicated through the product packaging that clearly reflects who they are and what they offer to their customers. RXBAR saw an opportunity in the market where others perhaps didn't. And it wasn't a bad one they spotted, considering that the brand was acquired by Kellogg for a reported $600 million in 2017.[31]

According to the company's website, founder Peter Rahal, of Lebanese descent, and his best friend started the company in 2013 when the CrossFit industry was taking off, with the goal to introduce a more nutritious, simple, and real food protein bar to a niche market—primarily targeting gyms as a start.[32] Both founders complemented each other as business partners from the start to create a protein bar snack that is considered to have clean ingredients, is gluten free and high quality, with little to no sugar (any sugar in the protein bar usually comes from the dates) that can accompany anyone on their wellness path.[33]

This product makes me happy whenever I'm standing at the grocery store, analyzing the ingredients of protein bars, or other products of the brand, to decide on the healthiest option to buy. Part of me still feels a sense of hope when I come across a product like this one with a short list of ingredients that I can pronounce. I like products that don't require me to grab my phone and look up half of the ingredient list while I'm clogging up the grocery aisle only to find out that something like titanium dioxide is in my food. Though supposedly considered safe in foods, this is the same ingredient that is found in automobile tires and rubber shoes. Not very appetizing, huh? The same goes for additives or artificial colors used for candy in the U.S. that come with a warning label or in some cases, are banned in European countries as these ingredients can cause all sorts of allergic reactions or hyperactivity in kids.[34] These should have no place in our food. To promote a safer version, you can find these same types of candy in Europe using natural colors that are found in fruits, vegetables like beta-carotene (orange pigment naturally found in carrots), or spices like turmeric. Why does it have to be so difficult to find products and foods that are healthy and nourish our bodies in the right way without having to spend hours on research to understand what we're putting into our bodies to begin with? And don't even get me started about the cosmetics industry that includes many of the same harmful ingredients that our skin, hair, and nails absorb.

Brands like RXBAR that are upfront about what they do and how they do it, earn the trust of customers because they keep it real and cite "healthy ambitions and usual insecurities" as the stuff that keeps them human.[35] Consumers are demanding better products and companies are providing them. When brands strive to make their products and food better, they tend to leave their customers better, too.

Just like Chobani ("shepherd" in Turkish), the brand known for dominating the Greek yogurt space, which underwent a complete rebrand in 2017 with the goal to expand beyond the yogurt category and position itself as a food and wellness-focused company, offering natural and nutritious food to make the world a healthier place. Started in 2005 by Turkish businessman Hamdi Ulukaya who immigrated to the U.S., Chobani is known as America's No. 1 yogurt brand, a product made with only natural ingredients without artificial preservatives.[36] You can't stand in the yogurt aisle of any grocery store and not notice Chobani but still, there was room for improvement to ensure continued brand relevance during a time when the company was in a leading position.

The rebrand jumped right at me when I was browsing the grocery store on a Sunday morning. I remember seeing it and getting excited because I knew immediately this was a rebrand done right. To continue to be a leader and innovator in this industry and the CPG category, a few things had to change and sure enough, they did. Many brands and competitors in this space seemed to use glossy finish sleeves with bright colors and textures, making it difficult to differentiate one brand from another. One of the first changes I noticed was the bold and fresh font compared to the old typeface and block-style lettering. The second thing I took note of was the dramatic improvement of the fruit ingredients on the yogurt cups, which made it more real and authentic looking without a doubt. It sparked memories of my Garnier Fructis hair care project at L'Oréal Germany, where the brand moved away from a manufactured fruit image to convey the shampoo ingredients on their product packaging. Introducing a more authentic look resonates better with customers and supports the new branding direction in a similar fashion as Chobani does. The previous packaging had perfect images of strawberries, blueberries, peaches, and other fruit, portraying an image that was too unrealistic and too perfect if you paid close attention. Instead, the new packaging introduces a more realistic, imperfect image of the fruit ingredients that are drawn or hand-painted, making it feel more natural. With this rebrand, Chobani successfully positions itself as a natural brand to continue to evoke the same ideals it originally set out to do when it launched in 2005.[37]

In Chapter 3, I shared how the personal beauty care brand Dove fosters self-identification through their efforts with women and girls. Dove is also one of the companies who continuously reflects authentic elements in their brand essence with real beauty campaigns that have allowed people to look at the brand as more than just a soap company. Campaigns as such that show people in all shapes, sizes, and colors seem to be the norm for Dove. This type of marketing aligns with the brand's focus around authentic and real beauty and to "only show people as they are, in real life, 100% authentic, 100% unedited and 100% beautiful."[38] To change the conversation around beauty, Dove is "on a mission to redefine, realign and make beautiful again. We've always stood for real beauty that's unique, diverse, and inclusive. And we want a world where beauty is a positive experience for everyone."[39]

By authentically championing body confidence and a positive experience with beauty, especially starting at a young age, Dove contributes to changing the narrative with their consistent message in positive ways. Conversations around beauty evoke emotions in girls and women alike who can relate to issues they feel strongly about that they don't have to tackle alone.

In the age of authentic marketing, it doesn't matter if it's in the food, fashion, or beauty industry, customers across various industries demand brand authenticity more than ever; brands who are real when deciding who they want to support. To make your brand more authentic and create valuable connections with customers in a more authentic manner, here are three things to consider:

1. Create strong brand values
   - Who are you at the core and why does your brand exist? What do you stand for? Your brand essence describes the emotional experience of your brand and presents a clear expression of who you are.
   - What are your brand pillars? These are known as the building blocks of your brand identity.
   - How are your brand pillars expressed? Tell customers what you believe. You can further develop your brand pillars by developing your brand promise and how to manifest this. When you deliver what you promise, customers know what to expect from you, so trust is earned.
2. Build strong relationships with your customers
   - What are your customers' wants and needs?
     - Create easy and clear ways to communicate with your audience. The feedback you receive from conversations or research should be incorporated into your messaging strategy that connects with your key values.
   - How can you meet your customer expectations by manifesting your brand?
     - Figure out how you want people to feel about your brand but more importantly, go beyond that and figure out how people want to feel about themselves. The way you define your brand should align with how customers perceive you.
3. Use your brand values to drive your products and/or services
   - How do you live out your values through words and actions that are reflected in your products or services?
     - Make sure to articulate the key values your brand offers by developing message frames to ensure your strategy reflects authentic ways to connect with your customers.

- How are you positioning your values and messaging per audience?
  - Define your expressions of the messaging framework to connect with your key audiences.
- Live up to your values.

As customers choose to do business with brands whom they perceive as authentic over the ones they don't, brand authenticity is no longer a choice but rather critical for any brand to endure as you develop your roadmap to success. A true emotional driver to making a purchase that can lead to loyalty and more revenue, authenticity proves to be more than a buzzword. Authentic brands enjoy deeper emotional connections with their customers who can relate to their brand the same way they relate to humans as they continue to be inspired. What matters is that you connect what you sell with what people need at the right moment in time—in the right way.

Love Notes

1. **Stay true to who you are**
   Honesty, reliability, transparency, truth, and trustworthiness are key elements of authenticity that will win the game. If you want to be taken seriously, you have to mean what you say and back up your words with action. When you make a promise, make sure to deliver on it. Consumers want brands they can trust in good and in bad times. Without trust, a love brand is out of question.
2. **Reduce negative sentiment**
   With a customer-centric approach, brands can show a strong level of caring in the right way and at the right time. Find ways to mitigate the negative sentiment around your brand.
3. **Demonstrate strong values**
   Build strong brand values and customer connections. Then, use your brand values to drive your offerings to reach your intended audience. People connect better with brands when they sense realness in the ones who live up to their own values.

05 Embracing purpose and sustainability

"Life without love is like a tree without blossoms or fruit."

KAHLIL GIBRAN

There comes a time in your life when you start to get tired of unhealthy relationships, even with brands who no longer serve your needs. You become intolerant of having them in your life. So, you go out and find new brands, new products. The ones that make you feel good, provide value, and understand who you are. The brands people seem to love more and more also love the planet. Sustainable, environmental, and social factors are becoming a brand's secret weapon to make meaningful impacts in the world as consumers continue to change and evolve, according to Talkwalker.[1]

Some brands look at their companies as more than just a business, more than buyers—a vehicle that can be used to drive change and communicate their *raison d'être* or reason for being. Airbnb promotes connection and the feeling of belonging. Whole Foods embodies pureness and nourishment that makes you feel good. So, how can you find the right balance between your brand and your cause?

I encourage you to think about your "why"—to look at purpose as your North Star. At Blended Collective, we go through various brand exercises with each client to find ways and adjectives to describe their brand and then slowly build the emotional brand experience that serves as the foundation to developing the rest of the brand. Then, we focus on the brand identity that encompasses the brand pillars and brand promise (what consumers can expect from your product or service). Thinking about ways these core values and promises can manifest through actions, allows the brand to convey deep and long-lasting meaning to customers. The intention of why the business exists is what drives all other elements when it comes to marketing and communications. To make the brand idea clear, we like to create one singular statement of what the brand represents and use this to drive all brand communication.

Inherently purpose-driven and sustainable brands stand out and are more memorable as they inspire like-minded people who believe what they believe to join them for the ride that goes beyond their brand offerings. Over time, purpose and sustainability have emerged to not only differentiate brands but to also bring about change that includes people because that's exactly what they are looking for—brands who enact change and move the needle. Naturally, the two are linked together because when a company aims to be sustainable, it's usually for a deeper reason. Globally, 71 percent of consumers want to adopt a more sustainable lifestyle.[2] But what does it take for consumers to willingly spend more on sustainable and purposeful products? It starts with the brand.

How Patagonia lives its purpose

Brands who operate with intention in everything they do are the ones who attract the right people. They're usually very clear in why they exist. Patagonia is one of the best examples and has staked its entire reputation on being a brand who lives its purpose with a clear and focused mission—from products and company culture all the way to its pledge to donate 1 percent of sales to the preservation and restoration of the natural environment since 1985.[3] I believe it strikes a perfect balance between purpose and sustainability by encompassing all three components: environmental, economic, and social efforts. Its values align with its actions from the way it sources suppliers, chooses materials, and even selects buildings for its locations. Patagonia is a U.S. retailer of outdoor clothing that was founded by Yvon Chouinard in the 1970s in California.[4] The company is highly intentional and authentic, one of the key emotional drivers of brand love next to the two additional ones of purpose and sustainability. When you have a mix of emotional drivers in one bucket, it makes it easier for consumers to move along the stages of trust and attachment in "The Eight Brand Love Stages," eventually leading to love and loyalty, too. To climb the ladder effectively, the brand and products must matter.

These days, many companies don't make great products anymore considering that they don't last as long as they used to. It's sad. The product lifecycles are becoming shorter and shorter, which means that replacing a product every couple of years or so is becoming the norm across many industries. It's a concept called commercial obsolescence. For Patagonia, though, long-lasting outerwear seems to have been an early goal and reality considering Yvon's passion for rock climbing, wanting to create products that last and can be cared for. Repair is an important part of the brand as it supports what the brand stands for by reducing the need for product replacement and protecting the environment at the same time. As I scroll through Patagonia's website at the time of writing, I can see a lot of educational information that spans climate goals, materials, environmental programs, and social responsibility.[5] This offers full transparency to consumers, so they know where and how the clothes they buy are made—the opposite of popular fast-fashion brands who are known to release toxic chemicals and waste in their clothing production facilities that are harmful to the environment. Unlike unsustainable fast-fashion brands, Patagonia believes in making high-quality products with a lifetime warranty for their customers that encourages them to keep coming back.[6] They offer customers ways to handle repairs themselves if they choose to do so by following the "DIY repair guide."[7]

Patagonia is not alone in wanting to reinforce quality. In late 2022, luxury fashion house Bottega Veneta announced a lifetime warranty program for their line of bags to ensure the longevity of their products.[8] When I see brands with such confident statements and offerings, it proves that they stand behind what they produce. They know that they produce good-quality products that are meant to last forever but in case they don't for whatever reason, the company is here to fix the issue. While I appreciate this, I also can't help but think, "as they should." I can't imagine paying for, or better yet, investing thousands of dollars in a designer bag and having anything happen to it with zero brand warranty whatsoever. Part of me feels like all brands who charge a premium price for their products should offer this, but you know it's too good to be true. Back to Patagonia—the brand is such a good example of living up to its own philosophy because its values align with its actions consistently, which allows for trust to be earned as well. Isn't the same true in our personal lives? We trust people whose actions align with their words that we can rely on.

Do you remember when, in 2011, Patagonia ran an ad in *The New York Times* on Black Friday, telling people, "Don't buy this jacket"? They were standing up against consumerism by urging people to think before they buy.[9] Patagonia's buyers and supporters have really come to appreciate the brand's efforts to stay true to who they say they are.[10] Basically, to fulfill their brand promise, the value or experience that consumers can expect from a brand every time they interact with that company.

Not only does Patagonia emphasize the actions it takes to make the world and environment a better place, but it provides education and solutions to how customers can be a part of this, too, strengthening community. For instance, fixing your clothes by hand or simply trading in products to receive credit. Even though functional benefits and quality come first for the brand, Patagonia can emotionally engage its customers with a deep sense of purpose that doesn't make them think twice about paying a higher price. By taking into consideration different philosophies such as about the product, production, distribution, marketing, finance, human resources, management, and environment, the brand creates a holistic approach to make sure it ties back every part of the business to its core values rooted in activism. So much so that founder Yvon Chouinard chose to go deeper into the company's purpose to help combat climate change by giving away the company as of 2022 to The Patagonia Purpose Trust and the Holdfast Collective (the 501c4), a nonprofit organization that aligns with his vision to continue the environmental support and justice goals, instead of going public or selling the company as most founders are known to do.[11] When you're a founder and stay in control of your company like Yvon Chouinard, it's easier to ensure that everything you do is done in service of your company as *you* choose.

Social activism, "one scoop at a time"[12]

Similarly, Ben & Jerry's is a company who has been in the forefront of social responsibility for a long time. Founded in 1978 by Ben Cohen and Jerry Greenfield in Vermont, the company now operates as a subsidiary of Unilever and still seems to maintain its core purpose.[13] The goal of selling ice cream has long been intertwined with the purpose of tackling problems and issues they care about. In short, they use their position to influence change for causes that are bigger than ice cream. Whether it revolves around voting rights, racial justice, LGBTQ rights, climate justice, campaign finance reform, or refugee rights, Ben & Jerry's is vocal about its stand on these social issues:

> We believe that business has a responsibility and a unique opportunity to be a powerful lever of change in the world. We can use traditional and contemporary business tools to drive systemic progressive social change by advancing the strategies of the larger movements that deal with those issues, such as climate justice and social equity.[14]

A flavor like *Change is Brewing* communicates this message clearly and in innovative ways by attaching a flavor of cold brew coffee ice cream with marshmallow swirls and fudge brownies to one of our most fundamental rights as humans—the right to vote.[15] In 2022, the flavor was rebranded to celebrate the power of Black voters to encourage people to exercise their power to vote.[16] The call to action on Ben & Jerry's website to encourage people to vote shows the intensity of involvement and passion the company has about the topic by dedicating an entire landing page to educate potential voters and allowing them to register to vote.

As customers, we might be curious about a company making the ice cream—we might want to know who they are, where they are based, and what they use to make the dessert. Do you, however, ever wonder about the environmental or social causes your favorite ice cream brand supports when you're standing in front of the freezer section in a grocery store? Do you think about whether coffee brands are sourcing their coffee beans in an ethical way and whether or not they have a fair-trade sustainability label? Maybe, maybe not, but this is how Ben & Jerry's seems to differentiate itself in this crowded and competitive ice cream category. The company stands out by emphasizing what issues they support through their words, actions, and creative product packaging, where other ice cream companies add not much else to the mix. It serves as a great example for others who want to lead with purpose and activism at their core. The focus of Ben & Jerry's is crystal clear—to lead with strong values with a commitment to their notion of linked prosperity at the center and equally balance an effort to make the world's best ice cream with profit while giving back to the global community.[17] Their ice cream might satisfy your cravings but it also makes you feel like you're contributing to society in a way that matters.

Speak up, step up

Speaking on social issues has become more and more important for businesses over the years, but the importance of this was heightened during the COVID-19 pandemic with economic hardships and social and racial justice issues like the Black Lives Matter movement, seeking to highlight racism, discrimination, and inequality experienced by the Black community. Other issues such as trade policies and immigration also encouraged brands to speak up during the Trump era—to the point of brands taking a political stand either voicing their support of then President Trump or not, influencing consumer decisions whether to continue to support certain brands and businesses. Brands need to be thoughtful in the social causes they support. It's not enough to only understand the benefit of supporting but one must also understand the risks when choosing not to. According to Edelman's 2019 Trust Barometer® Special Report, "In Brands We Trust?," 53 percent of consumers agree that brands have a responsibility to get involved in at least one social issue that doesn't directly impact their business.[18] The 2022 Trust Barometer® by Edelman shows that people want "more, not less" business engagement on societal issues.[19] In addition, restoring trust is key to societal stability, and the same research shows that providing quality information is the most powerful trust builder across institutions (business, media, government, and NGOs).[20] Brands should focus on ways to share fact-based information to build trust and while at it, master their emotions and not be so quick to react in the moment. Sometimes it's in your favor to take a step back and assess the situation before responding because once it's out there, you can't take it back. Timing is everything, but issuing a quick PR statement simply to say something is not always the best way to handle tough situations. By getting together with your team and understanding what the challenge or problem is and how you can respond by being sensitive to the consumer landscape, you're starting off right. It's not only about what your customers want to hear. It's about having a mindful, genuine, and sensitive approach to not further alienate anyone. How can your response show that you care? Responding in a way that doesn't only reflect your brand values but your customers' values can go a long way.

Intention vs. attention

There are brands who voice their support about social issues purely out of consumer expectations because by not actively taking a stand on any social issue, a brand is more likely to be criticized. This can be an issue of trust for customers, however. Adopting an approach to conduct business as usual with social issues present is probably not a good idea in today's world of marketing. Your business thrives on people who are paying attention and who want to encourage you to be part of the change. This is especially the case with younger people who serve as a critical audience. They want brands and people with influence who are in support of these brands, usually as some form of brand ambassador, to come forward and do what's right. Gone are the days when you could hide behind the curtain and wait for time to pass.

The socially conscious Gen Z population is one of the most racially and ethnically diverse compared to previous generations. They are also digital natives who grew up with little to no memory of what life was like without smartphones and, like Millennials, believe that climate change is due to human activity, as reported by Pew Research.[21] At a time when the bold cancel culture or call-out culture promotes the "canceling" of people or brands due to actions that are offensive or problematic, brands need to tap into their emotional intelligence, or EQ. With this, they can better manage and control their own emotions while being intentional about their actions. Nurturing our emotional intelligence starts with the consumer in mind, so it's important that we, as brand marketers, find ways to listen genuinely and spend time to learn and understand how they tick. Demonstrating emotional intelligence consists of actions such as being self-aware or conscious of the implications of what we say and do. We then have to manage all of it accordingly while displaying a sense of empathy, motivation for our actions, and social skills. When brands are aware of their words and actions and know how to self-manage or regulate when needed, it involves less trouble overall. We need brands who know what to say and when to act, displaying a good sense of their EQ that allows them to stand out among other brands and grow more successfully.

Live and breathe your purpose

The triple bottom line of people, planet, profit as I learned it in graduate school has transitioned to now also include purpose, and sometimes exclude profit altogether—at least externally for a business. If you want your customers to feel connected to your brand purpose, then you have to start internally above all else. I've come across too many brands who claim to have certain meaning and values attached to their brand along with the idea of who they want to be. The next thing you know, employees start posting the "real deal" on social media, explaining how the brand is not putting their money where their mouth is. Basically their purpose is just a front. Whew. Imagine what happens if, as a brand, you don't have your employees on your side to reflect, sell, and live your brand every single day in the best way possible. When they don't show up the way you want them to, it hurts. Yet, when your brand expectations are clear and you both show up for each other, there's no room for misguided expectations and it becomes all about reciprocity.

Your employees are your brand advocates on every level, helping you achieve success day in and day out. Without them, the journey will be much harder and frankly less exciting. As a brand, you need to bring your brand purpose and social sustainability efforts to life internally in the same way you intend to do externally because the true measurement of impact begins in-house. When your team understands and connects with your brand essence, you have someone who shares the same ethos as you and is eager to help you reach new heights—they're motivated by more than just a paycheck or salary. They are inspired by your mission. At the heart of every organization, every employee should be a brand ambassador. Not because they have to be but because they want to be. The truth is that employees want to see their employers take actions in the same way consumers do, and they want to be cared for. Whether this includes employee wellness programs or ways in which you select and treat your suppliers or partners you do business with to build stronger communities, every bit makes a difference. The same applies to diversity, equity, and inclusion efforts that have become ingrained across companies in recent years in a similar way as sustainability.

It seems like every brand I come across when I'm browsing through stores, wants to nourish their people and care for the planet by being more "eco-friendly." The same is true in the feminine hygiene market; a transition from disposable products to products that are more sustainable and organic is driving huge changes as consumers demand healthier products that don't harm their bodies or the planet.

It's so interesting to me when I'm shopping or just looking in general because when analyzing one segment of products on shelves, I can immediately tell in which direction the trend is headed. Suddenly, brands resemble one another more and more as they try to compete for market share and promote similar values they care about. It's most interesting when new brands arise in the marketplace that are sustainable from the moment they launch and are followed by others who have dominated the category for decades, not known for sustainability necessarily, but who suddenly present a line of sustainable products for the consumer group that cares and likely would abandon the brand for not doing so. It does make me wonder at times if brands who keep up do so because they genuinely care or if they're only jumping on the bandwagon.

With new tampon brands positioning themselves as "organic," "eco-friendly" or "biodegradable," consumers clearly care what they put in their body or what touches their skin besides the food they consume or the cosmetics they use. I remember growing up, topics like this among my group of friends were rather rare. Maybe because we didn't grow up with the internet as much, but even the access we did have to the web in our late teens was different. There was no YouTube influencer reviewing products or encouraging us to use one product over the other. For us, it was about flipping through teen magazines and word of mouth. Now, these conversations are everywhere and you can't seem to escape them. You can find social media influencers promoting healthier options and products that are plastic-free and non-toxic, educating consumers from a young age on what to pay attention to. Obviously, this is the case across categories of products and services. As a consumer myself, I care enough to spend a significant amount of time on research and ensure that I'm using the healthiest product when possible but frankly, it gets exhausting. Over time, I've trained myself to do it segment by segment as I'm replacing a product in my day-to-day life to avoid getting overwhelmed. From organic menstrual products to the honey I add to my green tea in the morning, where do I even start?

Customers care enough to want to hold brands accountable not only for what they do but how they do it and why. Is their product creation harming the environment, or our bodies and well-being, and thus the planet? Is there a reason why they exist beyond what they're selling to make a profit? When your intentions to follow such efforts are attached to your underlying business, it reflects a genuine attitude toward matters you choose to highlight in your business. On their journey, customers want to be accompanied by brands who make a difference in their personal lives and in the world we live in. They choose brands who are purposeful, ethical, and sustainable by either purchasing sustainable products or adopting such behavior in their everyday life.

Nurture your social programs

In my early days of working at a retail store, I was assigned to work in the shoe department, which was notorious for running frequent BOGO deals. Buy one, get one. You buy one pair, you get another one for free. Basically, you're getting two for the price of one. Who doesn't love that?

As a shopper, there's no doubt you already know this acronym, but over time, the "buy one, give one" model emerged as a new way to entice customers to purchase products. This model received just as much enthusiasm among buyers.

In 2006 and in subsequent years, TOMS is a brand who famously did this as a pioneer of this model. It felt like every other person owned at least a pair of casual TOMS shoes. The brand made a name not only for itself but also for its innovative commitment to give a pair of shoes to someone in need for every pair that was purchased. Impressive, huh? I can see how this would appeal to customers who especially care about giving back and were able to do so by also pleasing their need for a new pair of shoes. Giving back as a customer is simple. But giving back as a brand, at least in this capacity, maybe not so much. As of 2021, TOMS moved away from this one-for-one model. The brand found other ways to stay committed to giving by building meaningful partnerships with and providing impact grants to grassroots organizations who are helping to build equity at the local level.[22] Since their founding, TOMS has been known for its social impact and understands that it's important to take care of our planet. Their updated way of giving provides a more sustainable way to continue to offer best-in-class giving.[23]

Imagine you're a company with good intentions. When things don't seem to go as planned, though, it can really backfire. That's why it's important for companies to build a charitable giving strategy in a sustainable manner. To do this, brand marketers can consider various points including the supply chain and logistics impact to understand where the product is manufactured and distributed. For instance, are you producing your product in the same country you're giving it away in? Who are the best organizations to partner with that have the same high standards? What is the level of involvement of your nonprofit partners? And in the end, it pays to think about whether the giving away business model is truly making a difference as you envision. Giving might seem simple but the larger and quicker your business grows, the more difficult it becomes to make an impact that's sustainable for you to keep pushing forward. Consider Warby Parker, the direct-to-consumer (DTC) retailer of prescription glasses with a program in place that's embracing the "buy one, give one" model in clever and socially responsible ways.

Their "Buy a Pair, Give a Pair" program has been going strong to provide people across the world with access to vision in an effort to improve economic conditions and outcomes wherever and whenever needed. In fact, 1 billion people around the world live with vision impairment without proper care or access to treatment.[24] This statistic blows my mind and makes this initiative and commitment so much more relevant. As of 2022, over 10 million pairs of glasses have been distributed globally through Warby Parker's program, and since 2019 this work has been accelerated by the Warby Parker Impact Foundation.[25] It's clear that Warby Parker is dedicated to helping the global population in a tremendous way. I could go on and on about the different ways the company continues to impact people through the good work they do, but the point I'm trying to make is that whatever effort you commit to, you have to nurture it over time. I don't have the intel on how this program is managed in-house, but from what I've seen and read, it seems to be doing well and is enacting much change when it comes to vision access in many countries on an international scale. Of course, we don't know how initiatives like this will evolve over time and whether they will continue to be successful and impactful, or still socially responsible in the same way. Only time will tell. However, the key is to be realistic about what you can do, how you can do it, and many times, what partners you can do it with. You've likely heard the African proverb, "If you want to go fast, go alone; if you want to go far, go together." It doesn't matter if you're a small, medium, or large business. To enact positive change of this kind requires partners that support your social efforts and help you set the stage to grow such programs, or "scale," as entrepreneurs like to call it, in a healthy and consistent way. Creating an impactful initiative that people can stand behind matters, but what matters more is that you're able to keep up in the same way as it grows and develops. Just like a plant you nurture or children you raise into adults.

Empowering women

Whenever the name of fashion brand Tory Burch drops, it's synonymous with women's empowerment and entrepreneurship. Besides fashion, of course. I know other women-owned businesses that I'm connected to who feel the same way about it. The Tory Burch brand champions female entrepreneurs not only through the main fashion brand but also heavily through the Tory Burch Foundation that brings together a community of women. When I attended the annual Embrace Ambition Summit in 2020 in New York, topics like challenges, stereotypes, race, and gender were a primary focus. Before talking to anyone there, I could feel a strong sense of shared values in the room. In some ways, we all cared about entrepreneurship and empowerment. We cared about bringing issues forward by talking about them in the community to empower each other and start to enact change in small ways. In addition, year-round programs and resources are made available by the brand for women, such as fellowships, small business webinars, and intimate events I've had the pleasure of attending in cities like Chicago, hosted at Tory Burch stores—all while empowering women.

It was obvious to me that the brand wanted to take part and even lead these important conversations, both digitally and offline. Using a unique hashtag online such as #EmbraceAmbition as they do drives more awareness. Extending the use of this theme, or a key brand statement, in offline settings such as at events, keeps the conversation going. This annual Embrace Ambition Summit offers an opportunity for women to network and have conversations around meaningful topics.

Fashion brands who are driven by purpose like Tory Burch and position their mission strategically around causes to improve the world we live in, are the ones who end up creating the change—also because they naturally encourage others to come along for the ride not just for a season, but for a reason. Just like CVS Health did in 2022.

To provide easier access to menstrual products and support women's mental and physical well-being, health solutions company CVS Health launched an initiative called HERe, Healthier Happens Together.[26] "Period poverty," a term that describes inaccessibility to menstrual care products, hygiene, and education, is a real issue that is not often discussed in public settings. For CVS Health to step up and cut the price of period products by 25 percent, even considering paying customers' "tampon tax" in some U.S. states,[27] is a step in the right direction for what is an unquestionable necessity for women.

When companies as large and powerful as the ones mentioned in this chapter step up to address important issues in the community and have conversations that can make people feel uncomfortable but are necessary for change, it empowers others to join the conversation. In moments like this when brands embrace difficult discussions, they, too, show us that they care about social and economic challenges enough to choose to make a difference. Helping female consumers navigate these difficulties lets them know they're not alone. As a brand, you have to spend time to listen better and learn more, so you can continue to create a better world with intention. Time after time, brands have to move beyond transactions and tap into their purpose and the emotions of their consumers to inspire change.

Love Notes

1. **Go beyond transactions**
   Move beyond transactions and breathe emotion into your actions to inspire change. When you understand that it's not only about what you sell but why you sell it, you can create a deep, long-lasting connection that makes consumers feel emotionally rewarded.
2. **Commit to sustainability**
   Consumers show an increased demand for sustainability when it comes to products and lifestyles. When brands deliver on such desires, customers show loyalty in return.
3. **Listen and react**
   Consumers are looking to support brands who speak up and have a voice on issues they believe in. It shows that brands care and are willing to step up for what's right to create positive impact. Make sure to listen and assess the situation before you share your thoughts. Be mindful of how you express yourself.

Building trust and encouraging inclusion 06

"Do you think this is clean?" I find myself asking one of my vegan friends as I'm scanning my beauty and food products via a mobile app to decipher the ingredients and ensure it doesn't include anything toxic. It's not a secret that many products, even when labeled as "safe," can include harmful substances like chemical flavorings, additives, colorings, and other ingredients that consumers and some experts question. I'm less trusting of brands who choose not to be transparent about their ingredients upfront. Why make it so difficult? What are they hiding? The minute I spot a list of ingredients that takes what feels like an eternity to get through, it's game over.

In any solid relationship, too, trust is the foundation that provides a feeling of safety alongside that of other incredible possibilities. When you do what you say you are going to do consistently, you build trust. When we trust, we allow ourselves to be open and vulnerable with other people—we don't question what they tell us. We believe them. On the opposite side of the spectrum, every time we experience hurt in a relationship, we lose a sense of trust and have doubts as the relationship continues. It's similar with brands who disappoint us but if we trust a brand we love, can we, as consumers, go wrong? In "The Eight Brand Love Stages" model, trust is the stage where we move from brand desire to brand intimacy. It's the part where a crucial portion of the consumer-brand relationship forms that allows us to go deeper in how we connect. You can see that according to this model, trust takes several stages to develop but at this turning point in the relationship, it's a make-or-break situation. When you've come this far to earn the trust of your customers, you want to make sure to keep it. Without it, you're back to square one. When we talk about "trusting" a brand, it's more about trusting what we are being told is the truth; trusting the information a brand collects and shares with us. It's a building block where trust has to be given and earned.

In the early days of Blended Collective, I wanted to create a brand that connected with our audience while I hid behind the brand. Being such a private person, I didn't want people to know who was behind the brand or reveal my identity. I wanted to go for the mysterious brand vibe initially but looking back, I'm so glad one of my mentors strongly advised against it. In fact, thinking about it now, I don't know how I would have pulled it off in the long run anyway. The thing I was reminded of was that people do business with people who are behind the brand. They do business with people they know, like, and trust. They do business with us, with you, with me. You get my point here. I knew I had to put all my hesitance aside, trust my gut, and become the public face behind the brand. Starting a business and becoming an entrepreneur, you tend to eat, sleep, and breathe your business. Running a business in service to customers is a commitment we choose to make similar to committing to a new relationship. Sure enough, there is common ground between the two that requires two parties to come together to make sure this will work in mutually beneficial ways.

Doing the right thing

Showing consumers that they can trust the people behind the brand is key. In 2022, the 22nd annual Edelman Trust Barometer® report shows that businesses were more trusted than the governments in 23 of the 28 countries that were analyzed and that trust has declined for government and media to the point that business is the only trusted institution.[1] Meanwhile, government and media are both seen as divisive.[2] Interestingly enough, family-owned businesses are the most trusted type, followed by privately held, publicly traded, and state-owned businesses, respectively.[3]

Trusting a brand can include trust to protect data and privacy, trust to do the right thing, support the right causes, and more. When consumers understand what their data and information is being used for, they are more likely to share it without hesitation. Hence, when you collect data from your customer for a specific reason you state, it's important to follow through and use the data accordingly. It can be as simple as collecting email addresses for a newsletter on your website and as a follow-up, begin using these to send out the actual newsletter. I've come across too many businesses who have an email subscription option on their website but don't do anything with the information they collect. Concerns also exist about how companies use data without a consumer's true knowledge or consent. Both non-use and misuse of data can affect how consumers shape their trust toward a brand and have an impact on their engagement and purchase decision. For most consumers, across markets and demographics (i.e. age, income, gender) trust is a deciding factor or even a dealbreaker as they consider whether to purchase from a business.[4] In fact, 58 percent buy or advocate for brands based on their beliefs and values as of 2022.[5] For context, the 58 percent here denotes people who choose, switch, avoid, or boycott brands based on their values.[6] If you want people's trust in business, you must be cautious with the ways you choose to build it. Think about ways in which you can set a clear strategy for long-term success.

How HARIBO's special fan edition builds trust

HARIBO, "a leader in fruit gummies and liquorice,"[7] is a great example of a brand consumers want to and do trust. Trust is one of the six core values the company lists on its website and reinforces with statements like "HARIBO focuses on long-term relationships."[8] The company has a successful initiative with HARIBO Goldbears where it offers a special fan-selected edition composed of new flavors in the German marketplace. It's been such a hit that they now do this in other markets as well.

In Germany in 2016, I remember seeing brand messaging that clearly communicated that the trust of their customers is the reason for offering a fan edition. Putting the decision of flavor selection in the hands of their customers evokes a huge sense of trust both ways, specifically the flavor selection, which is incredibly important when it comes to a treat from HARIBO. Consumers have trusted HARIBO for years, so this campaign is unique in that the brand is turning to them. The brand is trusting them to choose unique flavors, such as apricot, grapefruit, blueberry, cherry, melon, and woodruff for the fan edition. Consumers are encouraged to visit the HARIBO website to cast their vote on their top six flavors they want to see on store shelves. Once flavors are selected through this online voting process, the final selections are produced and available to purchase at stores for a limited time.

In addition to HARIBO delivering on their core values, this initiative also emphasizes the importance of listening and responding to your customers. This was further highlighted with the Goldbears' 100th anniversary in 2022, when fans were offered entire bags full of their favorite flavor. They could buy bags of only pineapple, a massive fan favorite, and blue-raspberry, a new flavor.[9] To add an element of surprise and innovation, the company added one additional new flavor.[10] While these were part of a campaign, customers like myself can't help but wonder if these will become part of the regular product line, similar to Cadbury's Orange Twirls in the U.K. which were brought back as a special edition and, due to demand, seem to be here to stay.[11]

As a marketer, I pay attention to how brands communicate with consumers across all touchpoints and how they're delivering their brand promise (or if they do at all). The value of consuming such content and looking at brands through the lens of a consumer, too, is tremendous. I love being both. By allowing customers to be part of the process and soliciting their input, brands show that they care to make a difference in consumers' lives. And brands like HARIBO "want to continue doing what consumers all across the world like so much,"[12] to promote "childlike happiness."[13] Acting on their brand promise or core values creates a connection with consumers that results in a high level of trust being placed in these brands. Rarely is it enough to just tell people you can be trusted. You have to demonstrate it with something tangible. It's a no-brainer that building trust for a luxury brand as opposed to candy or shampoo is different. Building trust in categories like financial services or health care, too, is different than doing so for a food and beverage brand. However, one thing these industries all have in common is the fact that trust is essential on the journey to building strong consumer-brand connections.

Building trust across diverse audiences

I remember when in 2017, the hip Southeast Asian-inspired restaurant that had started as a food truck a few years prior and was voted number one in Detroit suddenly changed their name from Katoi to Takoi. What looked like a creative way to switch the letters "k" and "t" to come up with a new name after the restaurant was subject to arson and had to reopen a while after, turned out to be the result of the business being accused of cultural appropriation. The Thai word "kathoey" is offensive to Thai transgender people who face social and political stigmatization though they are widely accepted in Thailand, one of the most LGBTQ-friendly countries in East Asia.[14] Because the term can be used in a discriminatory manner, the restaurant owners whose aim was to create an inclusive space for the community all along but were unaware of the actual meaning of the word, listened to community feedback and chose to do the right thing—to be socially responsible.[15] Six months after the fire, the restaurant properly reopened as Takoi[16] and continues to win awards in Detroit.

Cultural appropriation describes a creative or artistic form that is taken over by an individual in one culture and used in another context.[17] The term has been called out more and more through social media and has garnered lots of attention through various platforms, as brands and marketers who are not part of a diverse community might try to benefit from another culture in a way that might seem exploitive and far from authentic. Being culturally aware and supportive means educating yourself about cultures and meanings, as well as celebrating multicultural audiences throughout the year, not only when it's convenient during cultural months such as Hispanic Heritage Month, Asian American and Pacific Islander Heritage Month, or Black History Month.

One way of educating yourself about cultures you want to reach through your marketing efforts is to tap into these audiences directly and efficiently. Of course, the easiest way of doing so is through your own employees and in-house staff who represent these very same cultural groups—or should. It has been shown time and time again, in both personal and business settings, that we as people connect with others who are like us and that includes cultural backgrounds in many cases, too. When consumers can see themselves in a product or brand from a cultural perspective, it resonates with them, and they learn to trust that the brand operates from an authentic point of view and is respectful and caring about reaching and engaging their customers in authentic and honest ways. Usually, you would think that businesses with fewer resources are the ones who fail to do the right thing but in fact, many times they are brands who have all the right resources you could imagine.

When I talk about companies who have the "right" resources, I'm referring to in-house brand managers or marketers who are culturally representative of the audience the brand is trying to reach. Your diverse team is your focus group. It might seem obvious that when working on a campaign with the goal of reaching one specific type of cultural group, you should at the very least invest in research that allows you to gather insights from this group to understand how your campaign or marketing efforts will be perceived on the other end. However, sometimes it doesn't seem to be as obvious.

Growing up as a child in Germany, I remember how movie names were generally adjusted in the German market, or other European markets. Sometimes they were adjusted to an English name but still different than the original. Looking at it when I was younger, it never made sense why American movies were released under different names, but after studying and stepping into marketing roles as I got older, it was clear as day. It's done to appeal to larger audiences and different markets in that culture. Different countries are also subject to different licensing laws and restrictions, which could have an effect, too. The same was the case with music videos and singles of U.S. artists who strategically chose which content to release in which parts of the world—another effort that seemed to tailor content and marketing to various geographic regions based on consumers in those markets. After all, a title should be understood and quickly resonate with most people. To do so, it demands the adaptation of titles and content. By understanding and integrating this type of knowledge, you set up yourself and your brand for success from the start.

Implement strong diversity, equity, and inclusion in your marketing

Unintentionally, brands sometimes make the mistake of being culturally insensitive only to issue a public apology later. According to years-long research related to ethnic and gender diversity by global consultancy McKinsey & Company, companies who are already entrenched in diversity, equity, and inclusion work are more likely to bounce back quicker and outperform any non-diverse companies when it comes to profitability.[18] The reason for this is that diverse teams have differences that shape their thoughts and contributions in their work life, too. Seeing the world through different eyes and coming together collaboratively, adds a truly inclusive way of solving problems and coming up with solutions. Yet, we live in a time where global brands are accused of not being diverse enough (or of racist attitudes in some instances) and are pushed by their consumers to move the needle in the right direction. There are too many brands to count who fall into this category. Many times, they're the ones you'd think would have enough tools and resources to make it happen, but time and time again, it's safe to say they don't have the right ones. Brands are slowly changing their attitudes to start listening for change to restore consumer trust again. Whether it's initiating in-house diversity and inclusion training or adding roles for chief diversity officers as the first step to head in a better direction, signaling the importance that's placed on DEI—both internally and externally. Over time, these efforts can translate into investments for community-based programs and scholarships to support minority-owned businesses and multicultural audiences. Creating diversity roles to drive this work forward is a great start, but it's not always the only answer and certainly not enough to walk the talk. Diversity and leadership accountability starts from the top and ideally should filter through the entire organization to effect strong and impactful change. It doesn't suffice to dedicate DEI resources to HR and call it a success. These efforts are crucial and should be woven into all departments across the board.

The benefits of diverse and inclusive teams are clear. Not only does diversity matter when it comes to the two most widely recognized factors—gender and race—it also relates to all other factors such as diversity in life and work experiences, and diversity in thought and perspectives, beyond gender and race. It's expertise that determines whether employees remain in the workplace and thrive. And when that's the case, representation of diverse, in-house talent leads to proper representation of diverse audiences. It sounds easier said than done but this is where it starts—investing in diverse teams who are impacting your marketing content. It's not to say that you can't be part of a team working on a project for an intended audience that you don't represent, but when teams are assembled who have limited to no cultural intelligence for the market they serve, it becomes a larger issue. This is where brands struggle and, in some cases, fail.

According to McKinsey & Company, with consumers becoming more inclusive they are more likely to do business with brands and in fact, trust the ones who show diversity in their advertising and marketing.[19] The same research shows that inclusive consumers place much emphasis on supporting small businesses and believe that there is a responsibility to actively support more Black-owned businesses and brands.[20] When you can make your consumers feel represented in your marketing, you make them "feel seen." Active acknowledgment shows that you believe that they matter. The same goes for companies who want to work with multicultural and diverse brands.

An inclusive approach to brands and procurement

In response to consumers seeking increased cultural support and to increase DEI efforts overall, both resulting in more trust when depending on consumer-brand relationships, brands actively engage in cultural heritage months to celebrate the heritage and history of cultures as well as the many contributions to community.

Take, for instance, the Minneapolis-based department store chain Target Corporation, one of the largest retailers in the United States. At the time of writing, their mobile app includes special content during cultural heritage months that's inspiring. During Latin Heritage Month, I came across content that encouraged visitors to shop for products from Latino-owned businesses.[21] Overall, visitors were encouraged to shop diverse collections to support diverse communities. Target's approach is admirable in that it targets not only customers but also various audiences, including business owners who might not realize they can "register" as a Latino-owned business, or a diverse supplier in this case, with Supplier Diversity in the company's portal. This shows support not only for customers to benefit the bottom line for the business but also an effort by the brand to recruit diverse suppliers.

Supplier diversity as business practice

Supplier diversity is a program that is a part of procurement departments at any company, typically larger ones who have the resources, assisting in sourcing diverse suppliers for a company to promote a more inclusive approach when it comes to procurement. As a diverse supplier, your business has to be 51 percent owned and operated by a minority group, which is classified as either a woman-owned business enterprise (WBE), minority-owned business enterprise (MBE), a small business enterprise (SBE), or owned by an LGBTQ, veteran, or disability group. Corporations place importance on third-party certification and effort in hiring diverse suppliers, which, believe it or not, does affect consumer behavior.

Remember when we discussed that consumers are more likely to support businesses who support diverse brands and small businesses?[22] Well, by incorporating and utilizing diverse suppliers, it helps diverse businesses grow, resulting in great economic impact on local communities, too. It's a win-win situation for everyone. Corporations meet their mandatory percentage to hire diverse businesses, and these diverse businesses are encouraged to grow and thrive. All of this while inclusive consumers continue to support corporations who care to add diversity to their supply chain and support both small and diverse businesses.

Many companies continue to place an importance on working with diverse suppliers across multiple functions, including marketing and advertising. "It's not an overstatement to say that supplier diversity in marketing/advertising is more important than ever. Investing in diverse suppliers helps a company's supply base reflect the customer population being served. It increases customer insight and drives innovation. And it provides direct investment to local communities. Supplier diversity is good business! But there are challenges," says Bill Duggan, Group EVP at the Association of National Advertisers (ANA), committed to supplier diversity and offering multiple resources to the marketing and advertising industry.[23] "Diverse suppliers see their biggest challenges to be getting their foot in the door with national advertisers or agencies, and lack of feedback when they don't get the business," according to Bill.[24] Meanwhile, advertisers and agencies don't seem to fully understand the value of using diverse suppliers and identifying opportunities to bring diverse suppliers into an organization's marketing or advertising supply chain.[25]

DEI efforts as such are also seen in the educational sector where colleges and universities have multicultural centers and departments for student voices to be heard. Efforts of this kind further extend into the financial sector like Morgan Stanley's in-house startup accelerator titled the Multicultural Innovation Lab. This launched in 2017 to promote financial inclusion and provide help to tech startups, offering access to tools and resources, mostly funding, so that founders with multicultural backgrounds can grow their companies.[26]

All of these industry examples display a strong effort that shows multicultural engagement across the board. It's not a surprise that a one-size-fits-all strategy no longer works. In acknowledging the cultural differences and engaging consumers in the right context, these companies and institutions are positioning themselves wisely and strategically for a future that is projected to be majority multicultural. This means that consumer loyalty will come heavily from multicultural consumers, so anyone who is not catering to this demographic already, or at least preparing to do so, risks losing out on opportunities. You want to be forward-thinking and innovative in your marketing approach, which also indicates that you understand your audiences and care to cater and communicate in a way that resonates.

The make-or-break moment

It takes time to build and gain trust. Trust is a fundamental value to any relationship, whether it's between individuals or consumers and brands. It can take years to build and five minutes to lose when a brand scandal emerges, or trust is violated. The same goes for a brand's reputation, which can be lost in a matter of seconds. Does this only hold true for brands whom we don't fully trust to begin with?

If we understand that behind brands are real humans, shouldn't we, as consumers, be more inclined to empathize with brands when they make mistakes? Brands can make mistakes just like people can because they're run by individuals. Why, though, is trust lost so quickly with a single corporate misstep? Is it because of the reaction of the company? Is there a secret formula depending on the circumstance? Will we always forgive them if they apologize for a mistake? Or should they try to brush small things under the rug?

To consumers, data privacy and trust in the financial sector matters more than in other industries. Knowing this, one of my clients, who is both a financial advisor and an estate planning attorney, quickly realized that in his industry where trust is crucial, advertising on social media is not the best way to win the trust of new leads. At least not in the traditional way by using text ads for his business. What he commits to instead is sharing fun and relatable videos he records with his young daughters at home where the conversation of estate planning comes up naturally, as they're playing "heads or tails" to decide who is going to take care of them in the case something happens to the parents. Showing his children getting frustrated with the current situation, each video ends with a unique hashtag #ThereHasToBeABetterWay and an online search for his services.

This personalized video ad content is short and sweet, gets the point across, and creates lots of regular traffic for him. Part of the reason this works is that it allows him to remain top of mind for his existing network of people who remember him when they have a need for his services because there's usually a sponsored ad video of his on their timeline. Another reason is that showing his family in the way he does is very relatable to the people in his network who are in similar situations—they're either newlyweds or have just had a child, making them ideal clients for the services he offers. All in all, he finds success when he builds trust before he mentions that he offers financial services. This works better than it ever could in reverse. This is specific to the financial service industry, of course. For those unfamiliar, consumers have to get to know a person in this space, feel comfortable with their process, and truly like the individual to be able to trust them with their money now and in the future. Company reputation for the products they represent helps too. Most of it, though, comes from building a trusting connection with the financial representative or advisor.

There are a few ways a company can lose the trust of customers; bad customer service experiences and declining product or service quality are two important ones. I can't even begin to count the poor customer service experiences that made me promise myself that I would never spend a dime with these businesses again. I don't care if they offer more convenient or cost-efficient options. It truly is one of the key reasons for losing the trust of a customer, especially, when the business refuses to admit their wrongdoing or fix the problem. If the brand violates the relationship and is no longer doing the job it's supposed to, customers feel more comfortable ditching the brand. In fact, they might even feel compelled to avoid it. When customers no longer believe in the brand they trusted or depended on, they sometimes are less likely to purchase due to feelings of betrayal. Let's keep it real. It's easy to never use a brand again because all you have to do is switch over to a competitor. But at what expense is your company willing to lose customers?

Love Notes

1. **Trust is a two-way street**
   Place trust in your customers by including them in the decision-making process for various marketing opportunities. Let them know you trust them as much as they trust you by developing ideas together.
2. **Ensure representation of diverse talent and suppliers**
   Companies should focus on hiring and advancing diverse talent in their pipeline based on various diversity factors to ensure they remain and thrive in their work environment. Sourcing diverse suppliers as part of the procurement process helps add diversity to the supply chain, which encourages inclusive consumers to support diverse and minority-owned brands.
3. **Deliver value to earn trust**
   Providing high-quality products and good customer service is important to build and uphold trust with customers.

Personalizing the customer experience

07

Personalized name chains are timeless to me. It's an interesting piece of jewelry to show some of your identity, or of others whom you cherish, and express your personality where your name can be featured in all sorts of different languages. Personalization of this kind is especially appreciated when you've spent years trying to find keychains or mugs with your name on them without any luck. Individuals like to be recognized as a person, an individual with unique traits, desires, needs, and experiences. We appreciate it when someone remembers our name—it's our human label. Consumers feel the same way we do when brands show them recognition in ways that show they understand who they are and what they need. In short, they appreciate it when a business recognizes them and caters to them personally because it shows that they're paying attention. Coca-Cola's popular "Share a Coke" campaign offered "personalized" bottles of the soda by including names on the labels. This is a fun personal touch, and many of my friends have fallen head over heels for this campaign.

Because of the level of personalization such brands offer, they have raised consumer expectations very high. Consumers are becoming accustomed to these personalized experiences like the custom Coke bottle, and they have come to expect the same level of personalization from other brands.

How MySwimPro built the #1 personalized workout app for swimmers

MySwimPro, the number one mobile workout application for swimmers, is focused on delivering a personalized swim training experience to help swimmers "live happier and healthier lives."[1] After all, people are inherently diverse. Why would a company assume that a swim program could be universal?

At the intersection of fitness and technology, MySwimPro was started in 2015 by CEO Fares Ksebati and his co-founders Adam Oxner and Mike Allon. Fares' role at MySwimPro was born out of his passion for swimming; he has been swimming since the early 2000s, swam collegiately at his alma mater Wayne State University in Detroit (my alma mater too!), and became an individual national champion. In addition to his personal swimming experience, his coaching experience spans more than 10 years. I sat down with Fares to discuss his experience and the journey to building his company. He said, "After graduating from college, I was trying to figure out how to fit swimming and coaching into my 'adult life.' I couldn't figure it out, so I started MySwimPro."[2] When Fares and his co-founders Adam and Mike identified a problem in the swimming community, they were quick to find a solution. The challenge was that people were desperate for swim workouts that matched their goals. Most people swim alone and feel isolated, longing for a community—quite different from when we learn how to swim as children, which is typically in group settings or teams. Then, in 2015, the MySwimPro app made it to the App Store and is considered the world's top fitness app for swimmers. Since then, MySwimPro's global and entirely remote team has grown to 15 people, and the app has reached over two million downloads, with 10+ billion meters swum, two million social media followers, and three rounds of fundraising.[3]

In fitness, the more personalized a swimmer's experience is, the more successful the training and hence the more likely the person will stick around. Personalizing your brand's products in a way that allows customers to create a closer connection with your brand leads to satisfied customers. "Swimming has had a transformative impact on my life and made me who I am today. I'm grateful for the opportunity to experience the water and help others swim," Fares shared.[4] A MySwimPro member, that is anyone who subscribes to the app annually, should feel as if they have a personal coach on their side 24/7 through the app; someone who listens to their goals, their skill level, and understands where they are in their swim journey. That's what a real personal coach does, although it's much harder to find this on your own in the space of swimming.

The challenge in the swimming market is that a lot of people swim because they can't do anything else due to physical limitations. When the pandemic caused swimming pools to shut down for a while, although it was quickly determined that swimming was safe and that the virus was not waterborne and hence didn't transmit through the water, the brand began to offer dryland workouts to democratize swimming. How is this different from other fitness brands and studios offering online and virtual workouts during this time? Well, MySwimPro's dryland workouts were specific to the sport of swimming. Fares explained how this helped alleviate some of the anxiety that increased for some people who couldn't swim but were used to doing so for mental health reasons, which, by the way, is truer for swimming than any other sport.[5] Members in the community had already developed strong trust in MySwimPro because the brand had been guiding them through their swim and workout journey. So, they continued to follow and hear about guidance during these challenging times. Instead of simply instructing members what to do, when Fares guided the dryland workouts from his living room, he performed the workouts with everyone, which helped the brand tremendously. The brand support was a result of the already existing connection and trust the community had built with him over time. Fares modified the workouts and ensured they were out-of-water programs that were specific to swimming. To further stay focused on swimming and ensure the brand maintained the subscriber base and slowed the decline, Fares hosted virtual events and a black-tie swim gala in 2020 that included Olympic Gold medalists Kaitlin Sandeno and Rowdy Gaines, known as the voice of American swimmers. Fares is confident that it's the social experience and community that delivers the long-lasting value for members.

Though Fares is at the helm of the brand and a trusted face that members are accustomed to seeing, he told me about a program MySwimPro used to run with a diverse group of global ambassadors.[6] The purpose of this program was for the swim community to further relate to global brand ambassadors on a more personal level. The brand found that swimmers connect to ambassadors who share similar reasons for swimming. For instance, someone's gender, age, location, or physique can all be factors that are relatable, but not as much as someone's reason for swimming. Some swimmers may be competing for the Olympics, others may be focused on losing 75 lbs, or simply building endurance and muscle strength—all personal reasons as to why a swimmer would want to seek out and connect with an ambassador where the connection happens organically in the Facebook group. As the brand and team continue to grow, so does their digital media and community engagement strategy. As of 2023, they transitioned the ambassador program to a more focused content creator program to better adapt to the evolving social media landscape. This allows them to continue engaging with the community while focusing their efforts on staying ahead of emerging media digital trends.

Swimmers around the world look to Fares for his expertise as it relates to coaching, advice, technique tips, and workouts. New swimmers in the community usually meet him as the face of the brand when they join. He's available to share technique tips on the MySwimPro YouTube channel, or his own, with continuous motivational efforts in the brand's MySwimPro Facebook Group with over 33,000 members as of early 2023,[7] of which about half are paying members. With 80–90 percent of content generated by the brand, boasting video-heavy content across the globe, only 10–20 percent of content is considered user-generated, specific content that is created by their network or subscribers instead of the brand. User-generated content as such tends to show high levels of engagement as it involves both the brand and audience. The brand gets to engage their following through social media while the audience gets attention from the brand it supports. It's the type of collaboration that proves to be a win-win for everyone.

In an effort to connect the swimming community even more, Fares co-founded an international swim day in 2018 known as World Swim

Day. This day is meant to empower people to swim while celebrating the sport of swimming and raising global awareness for learn-to-swim organizations.[8] World Swim Day is the philanthropic component of the brand that allows you to order a gold medal for $50, of which all proceeds are donated to swim organizations. The brand sees the most success with education-focused content compared to entertainment as it was initially created to solve a problem in the swim community and provide continued education in a swimmer's personal journey. MySwimPro has been so consistent with offering help and providing advice, that the brand has developed strong trust and brand reliability over time. With the addition of diverse content creators worldwide, the brand strengthens the rational driver of consistency, too. As you can see, adding consistent value over time, being agile and nimble when needed during challenging times, and marketing the brand "by swimmers, for swimmers," allows MySwimPro to build trust by doing everything they tell their community to do—with a strongly personalized touch. In short, they hold themselves accountable. It proves to be authentic, capitalizing on an additional emotional driver by practicing what you preach.

Personalization or customization?

Personalization is a great approach to build a loyal customer base that chooses your brand over and over again. As shown here with MySwimPro, it can help lead the way. What about Gatorade's "Gx Sweat Patch" that collects sweat from your workout and analyzes your sweat rate, fluid, and sodium loss, and helps you optimize your overall workout and performance with a corresponding app?[9] Or Hi Mastercard card holders who can personalize their card designs to feature their NFTs as of 2022?[10] So, personalization or customization? You might ask yourself, what's the difference?

Personalization meets an individual's needs by using their data to create or modify a product or service like Gatorade's "Gx Sweat Patch" example I just mentioned. Customization, on the other hand, is when the customer makes changes to their product or service to meet their own needs.

Starbucks is a good example I like to give because the company appears to focus on both the product and the service when it comes to shaping the customer experience. Don't you love when you walk into a Starbucks to wait in line and someone is standing in front of you, taking hours (okay, maybe not hours but a long time) to customize their order: "Can I get a Pistachio Coffee Frappuccino Blended Beverage Grande with almond milk, only two pumps of syrup, and light salted brown butter topping? Oh, and no whip cream please. And a drizzle of caramel syrup." And then I come along with my unexciting, unsweetened green tea order. But the exciting part of my order is the name I added to my account profile one time that now gets printed on the label of my order. I had listed my full name as Blended Collective to be funny and create some brand awareness when my name gets called when my order is ready at the counter. It was just for fun, but I left it and now it makes me smile every time it happens. Though sometimes the baristas get confused and accidentally think I want my green tea "blended."

I always think it's amazing how customized and detailed your beverage order can be at Starbucks—even when it comes to your name. Isn't this all part of what makes this global brand successful? I can adjust it to my liking whenever and however I choose to. And at the end, my cup has my name on it, or my company's name, to add a personalizing touch and fun to the entire experience.

Leveraging technology to deliver personalized experiences

I'm not a big fan of QR code menus, the digital version of menus at restaurants, which gained lots of popularity during the COVID-19 pandemic and seem to remain at most places as a contactless means to either look through a menu or, in some advanced cases, place your order. Personally, I like the experience of holding a menu in my hand. However, digital experiences are the cornerstone of new branding, especially when it comes to delivering personal and custom experiences. With continuous improvements in technology, data, and analytics, according to an article by McKinsey & Company on "The future of personalization—and how to get ready for it," personalization is going to be the key driver of marketing success for 2024.[11] And I'm convinced this will be the case for decades. When personalization directly contributes to marketing success in this way, brand marketers can create more personalized experiences across all consumer touchpoints. In considering "The Eight Brand Love Stages," strong personalized experiences not only lead to trust but they also help consumers advance to the next two stages of growth that includes attachment and, in some cases, love that consumers can feel toward the brand because of deep levels of understanding and empathy displayed.

How Oral-B's toothbrush uses AI to provide personalized coaching

The Oral-B iO toothbrush comes with an app that customers can use to track their brushing. The idea is that you can use the data to improve your brushing as well. Their built-in AI recognition guides customers through a detailed brushing experience. If someone does this wrong, the app will let them know with a sad face emoji. If that makes customers sad, maybe they will cheer up at the sight of their favorite light selection displaying at the top of the handle. This is my favorite feature as it indicates if you're using the right amount of pressure during brushing.

These intuitive responses make the brushing experience more personal. I use this toothbrush, and I feel like my product is getting to know me better day by day. One week into brushing with the app, I was able to see my personal brushing results, trends, and progress, so that I could keep improving them for better oral health habits. Receiving personalized coaching through a conversational display based on my own brushing behavior is next level, in my opinion. Oh, how I love the power of AI when it provides such value to my routine. It's products like these that make it easier for me to willingly give my personal information and data to the brand. It's even better when, as is the case with Oral-B, the brand has made its use and intentions with the data very clear. Their packaging focuses on how the data will benefit the customer, and it makes a big difference when the value-add is obvious.

Personalization is everywhere and can deliver immense value to both brands and consumers. Whether it's dental apps or menstrual cycle trackers that collect personal health data that is rather sensitive, brand marketers have to understand how to go about collecting and utilizing such data and analytics, and protect it, to implement personalization features in the most mutually beneficial way possible. It allows you to get to know and value your consumers on a deep level.

Love Notes

1. **Personalize with your consumer in mind**
   Do your best to use data and insights, so you can tailor your product or consumer experience accordingly. Personalization and customization both create value that naturally makes people want to connect with you on an ongoing basis, leading to deep engagement.
2. **Leverage technology**
   Utilizing innovative technology or AI helps you create a more personalized and human experience, which leads to stronger connections with consumers that make them feel special. In the future, they will only look for more personal experiences from brands, not less.
3. **Be transparent with data**
   Be upfront about how you intend to use data, analytics, and insights you collect from your consumers to personalize their experiences across multiple touchpoints. This level of transparency creates trust and leads the way to success as you show that you recognize and value them as individuals.

Being human and nostalgic 08

When we think of branding, the first things that come to mind are the visual assets because that's what our eyes are drawn to. Building on what I discussed about visual branding in Chapter 2, your brand needs to go beyond the visual identity to connect with customers in different ways that they can understand and appreciate. I'm not trying to say that a strong visual identity or design is not important because it is, yet in the world of marketing and with our five human senses that we sometimes take for granted, brands can choose different ways to show up and connect with their consumers to create deep experiences across various online and offline consumer touchpoints. As a brand, you should do your best to brand beyond your logo, beyond your visuals.

When branding and crafting your messaging, think about what your audience truly needs from you besides your product or service. Apple finds ways to connect people's emotions to new product lines year after year. Tesla's consumer feels that it's worthwhile to support the environment and sustainable energy. And when you see a Nike commercial, it's almost never just about the shoes; they often reference performance and evoke emotions, leaving people motivated and inspired. In short, there's always a story that revolves around emotion and what people care about. The brands who capture the hearts of their consumers and benefit from it, focus on more than what they offer.

As you read this chapter, I ask that you consider what emotions, values, and ideas you can offer your audience. What do you want people to walk away feeling when they interact with your brand? What sort of value are you offering every time they engage with your brand? What is your consistent brand promise to them? What memory are you creating?

Because we live in a very crowded marketplace, we have to differentiate ourselves from the crowd. One way of doing this is to tell a story that is unique to who you are as a company. Create your narrative to share your brand's history, challenges, successes, and value propositions—no other brand can copy YOUR story. People love a good story and what it stands for. And as you're telling your brand story, think about what makes you more human. How do you touch and transform people's lives? How do you make a positive impact on society? You can choose to be the brand who is more human. People will feel this, connect with you, and buy from you instead of a competitor. All in all, successful brands are the ones who know how to evoke emotion time and time again—sometimes by appealing to our five senses.

Mastercard's five-sense marketing approach

To adapt to a digital environment and continue to evolve, Mastercard dropped its name from the iconic symbol that is made up of two interlocked circles, red and yellow.[1] In my network and circle of brand marketers, the move certainly sparked lots of conversations. Just like Apple, Nike, and Target, the brand is now a part of an exclusive group that doesn't use the brand name in the logo. Frankly, these companies all offer something practical and of such immense value with great awareness that they don't need to have their name in their logo.

Since their iconic brand update, I see Mastercard everywhere. And it feels like the company keeps getting my attention for all the right reasons. They continue to push their forward-thinking approach further. I've seen them adapt their marketing with multisensory brand experiences that appeal to all five senses to deliver a holistic customer experience. Such initiatives include Mastercard's innovative Touch Card, a card specifically designed with unique notches to help blind and visually impaired people differentiate their cards when they're making a purchase.[2] The brand tapped into the sense of taste by opening Priceless restaurants around the world.[3] Or even the sense of sound through their sonic brand identity, which includes a music album called *Priceless*, so people associate the company with features outside of the logo.[4] Mastercard's brand strategy around the five human senses seems to focus on building meaningful products or experiences that help connect with their consumers on a deeper level.

Sense and emotion work together to create memories

In 1993, neurologist and founder of the Smell and Taste Research Foundation Alan Hirsch placed identical pairs of Nike shoes in two different rooms.[5] The only difference between the rooms was that one was scented and the other was not. So, what came of it? An overwhelming majority of the subjects said they would buy the shoes in the scented room.[6] When I first learned about the concept of olfactive branding or scent marketing, a branding strategy that consists of creating custom scents for brands and spaces to improve the brand image, I was unaware of its immense power and influence.

Sense of smell

While I was at a boutique store in Medellin, Colombia during my visit in 2022, I was pleasantly surprised by the way the sales associate bagged the product I was purchasing. She took my piece of clothing and put it in a nice, cream-colored cotton bag that seemed like it was specifically designed for the piece I was purchasing. She then took a scent, sprayed the piece here and there, and tucked it into the beautifully designed cotton bag. Voilà! Of course, I knew what she was doing. As someone who loves this sort of personal touch from a brand, I asked her about it anyway to see how she would respond. She said something along the lines of it being the store's signature scent and that they do this because they want customers to remember the scent when they unpack their item at home.

Have you ever wondered what your favorite brand would smell like if converted to a scent? My first exposure to olfactive branding was at Abercrombie & Fitch retail stores. Are you familiar with the scent of the space? It hits your nose the minute you enter the store. I don't know about you, but a good scent makes me want to spend money the same way I want to spend money when I'm browsing at a store that's playing music I love. Back then, I personally don't recall any other retail brand being as bold as this one with its scent in a physical store—besides stores known for selling scents, that is. I was excited to browse the clothing section because the scent was so desirable. A whiff of something can bring up a memory we didn't even know we had, and make us feel nostalgic if it's something we haven't experienced in a long time.

Years later, I walked into a hotel and was struck by a new scent. It was the type of scent that I knew would trigger years-old memories down the road. Hotels are known for "scenting" their spaces. Spas also commonly do this. The scent alone usually makes me want to go back to the space I associate with it because it ends up creating good memories. While sitting in that hotel lobby, I realized that brand identity clearly is not limited to verbal or visual senses. There's strong power in branding spaces with unique scent identities, a concept many of us have probably been exposed to subconsciously. Verbal and visual branding experiences actively appeal to our brain, yet others, such as olfactive branding experiences, may be more subconscious, as we don't naturally tend to connect scents with brands unless it's a fragrance brand. The most memorable experiences seem to be the ones that appeal to our senses.

Smells are first processed by the olfactory bulb, which is connected to parts of the brain that are strongly associated with emotion and memory.[7] Both smell and emotion work together, as smell triggers memories and emotions.[8] It automatically connects scent and emotion, creating scent memory for us—the most emotive of all senses.[9] Therefore, it shouldn't surprise us that brands use custom scents for their products or spaces as a mechanism to market to consumers with the aim of generating more revenue and creating brand loyalty in the long run.

Before scent marketing was popular, it seemed like it was simply attained by spraying the perfume or brand's signature scents throughout the store, adding uniqueness to the space. Scent marketing has been sought after at restaurant chains, retail stores, and hotels such as the Armani hotel in Dubai. When I visited Dubai for the first time in 2017, I quickly observed that scent branding was not limited to these spaces whatsoever. Scent branding was ubiquitous; not only in these permanent spaces, but also at temporary locations such as events and pop-up shops. Uniquely branded scents like I describe, create brand associations and memorable experiences for people, resulting in emotional and positive effects on brand strength that intensify brand loyalty. In the UAE, I immediately recognized Oud, a scent made of woody nuances, characterized by its strong smoky fragrance, traditionally worn by Emirati men and women. Indeed, it's so popular that I spotted plenty of western perfume brands with variations of this signature scent present in Dubai, some also adding musk as another key ingredient. Whether it's Giorgio Armani, Christian Dior, Gucci, Roberto Cavalli, or Yves Saint Laurent, the oil scent has become a part of fragrance collections across the Middle East that I came across everywhere I shopped. With this, brands localize their product offerings through scents. Attracting consumers in this market through these types of localization allows brands to generate more revenue while also offering exclusiveness in luxurious markets like Dubai and Abu Dhabi.

Scent as a differentiator

Over the years, brands have come to recognize the power of olfactive branding, or scent marketing, more and more. These scent elements are powerful ways to make us feel good and build stronger connections with brands even when we don't realize it.

Brands have become and want to be global, which has created a need for globalized scents. I can imagine the difficulty of trying to create such scents, having to analyze the different emotional attitudes to understand what people aspire to, the functional expectations to understand what they seek, and finally the sensorial expectations to know what people might be interested in. What a challenge to find a happy medium and product across all cultures that works for everyone. To create a strong product and proposition, you need to consider multiple layers when it comes to consumer needs.

It's clear why olfactive branding is so powerful. With the right scent identity, you can trigger engagement and affect consumer behavior in the right way for your brand. This contributes to the emotional result, which helps differentiate your brand while creating a pleasant customer experience.

Most business owners seek brand longevity; they want their brands to last for a long time. Not only is it challenging to create a new brand and associations from scratch, but consumers don't always like rebrands. Sometimes, though, rebranding or repositioning becomes a prioritizing thought and has to happen to modernize the brand or simply to stay on track with the way you're evolving. But when you have to recondition a consumer's mind as to what associations should be made regarding your brand, on average, this tends to be more difficult and costly than positioning a brand from the start and retaining your customers. The goal of olfactive branding is the same as visual branding when it comes to brand development. The brand has to communicate the desired message to the end consumer. Still, it takes time to get consumers on board with a rebrand. We hear it all the time: "People are resistant to change. People don't like change." It's because people like stability. It makes them feel grounded to know what to expect from you.

As a brand, you should think twice about whether you want to disrupt the consumer-brand connection and reinvent yourself. Knowing who you are without having to hit the restart button to get to know you all over again can hold power, too. With olfactive branding, the goal is to trigger the memory of consumers with a branded scent. If you change this scent, eventually the emotional connection and loyalty that customers have with a brand could reset. It's up to brand marketers to create new bonds and triggers. For a frustrated customer, this might justify a move to a new brand. And why would you want to create this opportunity for them to leave you?

How Sfumato Fragrances creates ties between fragrance, science, flavor, and experience

After noticing that scents have culinary ties, husband and wife Kevin Peterson and Jane Larson began hosting scented pop-up dinners around town in 2015. Shortly after, the couple began pairing their dinners with music and drinks to create a well-rounded social experience. When one of the guests approached the two about turning this idea into a business in one of his buildings, a new idea was born. The two co-founders didn't envision this could be a full-time business, but it took a life of its own by birthing two brands—a retail shop and a bar, namely Sfumato Fragrances and Castalia, respectively, both based in a Victorian mansion in Midtown Detroit in Michigan. Sfumato Fragrances is a niche perfumery producing natural and botanical scents, including unisex perfumes and colognes, incense, and custom perfumes.[10] *Sfumato* is an Italian word that translates into "turned to smoke, or vapor," which is what happens with one of the brand's fragrances the moment the scent leaves the bottle.[11] Kevin blends the compositions by engaging olfactory skills polished in the culinary world, which also fuels his passion for combining different ingredients. His email signature describes him as the "Co-founder, Nose and Cocktail Scientist," whereas Jane uses her background in art and design to create the visual aesthetic for the brand.

The store's architecture is designed so that by day it functions as a retail shop and by night as an experimental craft cocktail bar, Castalia. The space features wooden shelves with scent science and food-inspired books for customers to purchase. This is one of my favorite brand concepts I've seen. It conveys a distinct, intimate vibe and with the space housing fewer than 25 people at a time, it creates a cozy, harmonic feel. You know you're going to have a good time there no matter what. Usually, you end up in conversation with the couple next to you, inquiring on their drinks and scent flavors. Focusing on this concept between flavor and fragrance, each of the drinks is inspired by Sfumato's natural fragrances and is then paired with the scent. While in conversation with Kevin, he shared, "We've taken scent for granted, but it's a very emotional sense and it's underrated.

In the digital world, there's no way to digitize scent, so vision and hearing get top billing. We forget how important scent is, but it was highlighted during the COVID-19 pandemic when people lost their sense of smell and realized how many emotions are tied to it."[12]

To continue to push the boundaries and link these different worlds, Sfumato Fragrances creates new experiences through brand activations such as the one with the Detroit Symphony Orchestra (DSO) in 2018 for one of their events, Mysterium.

A multisensory experience at the Detroit Symphony Orchestra

The DSO's vision is to be "an inclusive and culturally relevant community where all people can experience their world through music."[13] At the time, the DSO's NextGen program combined a ticket membership program and volunteer leadership committee to attract and engage young professionals and develop its next generation of patrons. When NextGen hosted its second annual signature event, Mysterium, the concept for it was inspired by the unfinished work of the late Russian Romantic composer Alexander Scriabin to create an experience for the audience that engaged all five senses to create a state of enlightenment.[14] Scriabin was influenced by mysticism and imagined a synesthetic musical experience that would incorporate the sensations of touch and smell in addition to sound.[15] The unfinished piece left room for plenty of creativity in terms of what form it could take when performed. With the aim of creating a multisensory event with experiences to stimulate all five senses in creative and innovative ways, the strolling performance comprised three different intimate experiences, including one in Orchestra Hall, to include different genres of music from classical to jazz and pop, performed by DSO musicians. These musical and visual experiences in spaces throughout the building were accompanied by food and drinks, blending with the music while invigorating different senses for each experience, though the sense of sound was present in all, as you can imagine. One experience featured ballet dancers to focus on the sense of sight. While the music and visuals were taken care of by the DSO, Sfumato Fragrances became a sought-after partner to imagine and create the scent component in one of the spaces, evoking emotion in attendees throughout the evening.

Scriabin's vision of the piece involved his audience being taken to a mountain in India where everyone would gain enlightenment during his performance. "Nijananda," an already existing fragrance by Sfumato Fragrances, "encompasses Indian scents and presented itself as an ideal foundation," paired with a drink named Transcendence for the event, "of scent to accompany this classical music piece," Kevin continued to tell me about the brand activation.[16] "Many in the audience experienced scent and cocktails in this combined fashion for the first time," he added.[17] While it was a subtle experience for some, others were in complete shock to be able to approach and experience both smell and taste in this unique way simultaneously. The people in the audience were encouraged to wear sleep masks to cover their eyes, intensifying the experience of sound, smell, and taste. Not everyone was game for wearing a sleep mask, but the ones who did had a picturesque facial expression throughout the performance that was captured beautifully in event photos. The first sip, the sound of beautiful classical music in a room that was fully engaged, was a memorable experience—one in which all senses came together in an impactful way. With these worlds being inextricably linked, Sfumato Fragrances continues to expand its product line to enrich experiences and create memories through scent, such as incense, candles, and other custom projects—also with its sister company Castalia.

Amplify your brand with memorable sounds

I remember growing up when ringtones were seen as a cool way to let people know your music taste the minute you received an incoming call. It was part of popular culture before the smartphone life. While custom ringtones still exist, it seems as though they are rare these days. I know when I hear a custom ringtone, it typically leads to an eyeroll where I think to myself, "Does this person really have a custom ringtone on their phone?" Nowadays, this type of technology is more commonly used for "on hold" music as someone is waiting on the line. Sometimes it gives you the option to choose the music genre you prefer like jazz, classic, or pop. The same way I asked earlier what your favorite brand would smell like if it had a scent, isn't it fair to ask what your brand would sound like? The influence of sound can't be denied. You connect to a brand in different ways and audio is one of them. It doesn't have to be a brand that's specifically a sound-based product.

Sound has an effect on our cognition, perception, and behavior. According to Steve Keller, Sonic Strategy Director for Studio Resonate/SXM Media, sound is the "most undervalued sense in marketing."[18] As Steve puts it, "We don't talk about audio enough when it comes to branding."[19] Just as with other elements of sensory marketing, audio can help a company appeal to the emotions of consumers if used correctly and implemented strategically.

Budget might not always support sonic assets, but a lot of companies do benefit from a sound. Just think about the sound your computer makes when it turns on and how iconic that sound used to be. Imagine your notifications on your computer or your phone when unlocked—there are sounds associated with these. Audio is sometimes the last thing advertisers think about in the creative process, but that doesn't diminish its importance.

In a conversation I had with Steve while writing this book, he said that, "Audio doesn't start with your ears; it starts with what's between them."[20] Just as visual brand identity encompasses style guides for how to use a brand as it relates to the typography, colors, and logo, Steve encourages companies to think about creating a sonic style guide to help brands develop consistency in how they use audio assets across their brand ecosystem.

When it comes to creating distinctive sonic assets, Steve cautions against building a sonic identity on licensed music. It's dangerous to build equity in a property you don't own. If at some point you're no longer allowed to use the licensed music for whatever reason, you lose the equity you've built. It's no different than renting a home that's not yours, where you invest time and energy over the years but then are asked to leave by your landlord for whatever reason. It takes time to develop strong associations between a brand and a particular piece of music or an audio mnemonic. You want to make sure that the time and money you spend to create those associations contribute to your bottom line. Not the bottom line of some other copyright owner.

The key to developing a strong sonic brand is consistency. Brands need to create consistent sonic experiences across all the various audio touchpoints in their brand ecosystem. How do you develop and implement a sonic identity system? We've created a brand development process at Blended Collective that allows us to streamline the process of brand building. During my interview with Steve, we talked through our approach and came up with a reconfigured version that includes sonic elements.[21] Here are the steps to consider:

Step 1: Brand audit/assessment

The first part of the process involves doing a brand assessment and audit to understand the state of the brand. This is where we look internally at the foundation that the brand is built on, such as the mission, vision, and purpose. We also look at the brand externally to analyze its position in the marketplace. When it comes to sound, you want to pay attention to whether you can own a particular sonic space, one that isn't owned by your competitors.

Step 2: Research

This is where we conduct both industry and non-industry research, which includes a competitive analysis. When you're analyzing competitors to get a better feeling for what others are doing, I can't emphasize enough the importance of looking outside of your industry vertical too. In the case of audio, doing a competitive audit to see what sounds others in your industry are using (or not using) is beneficial.

Step 3: Brand discovery and development

During this stage, we spend time in group sessions or workshops that are specifically designed to help us build a profile for the brand. Getting to the core of "why" a brand exists and how it operates is crucial. Without this "why," it's difficult to lay claim to any kind of brand distinctiveness or purpose. Once the purpose is clear, we work collaboratively to make sure we're aligned on the brand attributes, both from an internal and external perspective. I'm not going to pretend branding is an easy job. It's tough. It takes a considerable amount of time and resources to be thoughtful and intentional when building a brand over the long term.

After the brand values and attributes are further developed, we're able to see patterns emerge that eventually become part of fundamental perceptions of the brand, further defining its core values. These values can then be turned into actions that bring the brand to life, allowing you to engage with your target audience, building and growing it. I love this part of brand building because it's so creative and allows my team and I to bring out the deep meaning of a company. Working with founders and companies through this process, you can see how much thought and creativity they've invested in building their brands—and how many of them have similar struggles, regardless of their brand category: "How do I communicate who we are in the right way? How do I tell my story so that it resonates with the people I'm trying to reach?" You can spend time discovering the brand with your marketing team or consultants, but never underestimate the power of workshops and focus groups that allow you to dig even deeper into consumer perceptions of the brand, offering an opportunity to gather even more insights.

This process ultimately allows you to build a sonic profile for the brand, translating brand personality, values, and attributes into a sonic language. What are brand archetypes? What are the brand colors? How can we communicate these elements with the building blocks of sound? What are tempos, pitches, modalities that connect to the brand? This process results in the creation of a detailed sonic brand brief that designers can use to start creating prototypes.

Step 4: Brand strategy and positioning

One of the goals of any brand strategy is to create a distinct perception of your brand in the minds of consumers. Ask yourself questions like, "How am I showing up in the marketplace? How does my presence differ for each one of my target audiences? How am I delivering my brand promise?" Your brand should be clearly defined, and your competitive advantage or unique selling point clearly communicated. Brand positioning is about ensuring that you align customer perception with brand intent. This is true when creating distinctive sonic assets for your brand, making sure that the sonic experience is consistent whenever, wherever, and however your brand is heard. How do your sonic choices reflect your brand across multiple customer touchpoints? When you're able to align your brand sound with other brand identifiers in a way that "fits" the brand holistically, creating mental availability and salience in the mind of the consumer—that's successful sonic branding.

Step 5: Creative

With your brief in hand, you can turn your attention to the next part of the process: creating prototypes of the distinctive sonic assets that will ultimately form the core of your brand's sonic experience. In the same way that visual designers translate a brand essence and identity into distinctive visual assets like logos, fonts, and colors, sound designers and composers generate the brand themes, sonic logos, and functional sounds that will ultimately represent the sonic identity of your brand, using sound to shape consumer perception and behavior.

Step 6: Implementation and measurements

Once the prototypes are created, you'll need to narrow down the design options. This typically begins with an internal review process, after which you can put the top two or three contenders into market research. The good news is that audio testing has become much more sophisticated and reliable, using both implicit and explicit methodologies that can give you a good take on how your sonic assets will perform in market.

A brand's sonic journey doesn't end with the creation of distinctive sonic assets. Creating the assets is a meaningless exercise if the brand doesn't use them in market. It's important that your sonic assets are used as often as possible, as consistently as possible, and in as many contexts as possible. As Steve puts it, "It's one thing to find your voice. It's another thing to see a return on your audio investments."[22] He encourages brands to develop "sonic KPIs" that drive to three specific pillars that should be at the heart of any sonic strategy:

1. *Consumer behavior.* Consider the behavior you're targeting and how sound can help you reach your goal.
2. *Consumer perception.* Think about how you want to drive consumer perception of your brand and how you're making sound choices to do that.
3. *Equity.* How can you use sound to build brand equity over time? In addition to brand equity, distinctive sonic assets can be trademarked and copyrighted. Building equity in the intangible assets themselves can allow you to collateralize the sonic assets over time, even generating royalty revenue that can offset costs.

Ultimately, success of an audio brand depends on two things. First, how well the sonic assets have been designed to reflect a perception of the brand that aligns with brand intent. Second, how disciplined the brand is in creating a consistent sonic experience whenever, wherever, and however a consumer "hears" it. Leaning into the flexibility, sound provides ways to optimize your sonic identity system over time. Rome wasn't built in a day, and your sonic brand identity will need time to connect in market. But once it does, we see from research that sonic cues are one of the most effective ways to capture mental availability, nudge consumers, and connect buyers at critical points of sale.

Wrapping up our conversation, Steve suggested that brands can increase the likelihood of success by focusing on six measurable parameters when creating, testing, and evolving the brand sound: "Your sonic identity should fit your brand, be memorable, distinct, flexible enough to work in a variety of contexts, appealing, and allow you to control the audio masters and copyrights."[23]

How Toyota's car model is humanized by having a soul

In the way that Spotify disrupted the music industry and Netflix disrupted the pace at which we consume seasons of television, autonomous driving is disrupting and reshaping the future of the auto industry. According to developments and conversations with automotive strategy experts over the years, it appears that the intelligent cars of tomorrow won't be just machines as autonomous technology has the potential to disrupt vehicle ownership—they will be something you have an emotional connection with. One of the brands who does this best is Japanese automaker Toyota.

Toyota uses AI to tap into human emotion[24]

In 2019, I attended the annual Detroit Auto Show, also known as the North American International Auto Show (NAIAS), and had a first glimpse on media day. Many automakers and new models caught my attention, but Toyota's Concept-i series inspired me to spend a significant amount of time admiring their brand display more than any others I saw that day. It was unique and stood out to me because it was visually appealing and creative, highlighting the car's emotional journey and core values. Toyota's vision of creating "partners in mobility" describes an emotional link between the driver and the car through artificial intelligence and mobility. This car series evokes an emotional feeling that makes driving fun, safe, and engaging. The name Concept-i is a play on the Japanese word for love "ai," which, in English, is pronounced like the letter "I." The term "Aisha" in Japanese translates to "a car that is loved."[25] Things that move our heart, such as meeting new people and having new experiences, are all opportunities that cars can provide through mobility. This cultural play on words seems to mirror Toyota's belief and desire to instill its future intelligent cars with an emotional connection to the driver, rather than treating them purely as a machine or vehicle.[26]

To support this, Toyota's vision is reinforced by this car's tagline, "More than a machine, a partner. Learn. Grow. Love." It also displays technology and core values to protect, learn, and inspire. "Protect" refers to learning about people and automated driving in a way where the outside situation, as well as the driver's condition and reliability, are continuously monitored. This is done by switching from manual to autonomous driving when needed for safety. "Learn," the second core value, explains that innovation occurs from learning about people. Learning about the driver's emotions, alertness, and facial expressions, allows for a more comfortable driving experience. The last core value, "Inspire," involves an agent, the female Asian voice named "Yui," who learns about the driver's tastes and individual preferences. For instance, the car understands that driving on congested roads where the driver is exposed to accidents can cause a feeling of irritation. Therefore, the car would suggest taking an alternate route to create a feeling of happiness. Connecting emotions to location information and subsequently using them as Big Data, is referred to as Toyota's *Emotion Map*. So, how else does Toyota evoke human emotion with its Concept-i model?

To emphasize the in-depth connection between the car and driver, the car is described as having a "new soul," adding a strong element of brand humanization. The more time the car spends with the driver, the more attached it will be, similar to how our feelings develop for people we spend more time with—recall the evolution from brand liking to brand attachment described in Chapter 1 as part of "The Eight Brand Love Stages." But does this suffice? Not quite. What about trust? Yui gets to know you through conversation and by reading your emotions. She ensures you're safe while enjoying the ride and is there for you whenever you need her, customized to your individual tastes and preferences. Looking at previous marketing campaigns and advertising, emotional branding is not new at Toyota. The brand's car and visual display at NAIAS was a phenomenal alignment with this marketing strategy by utilizing wording such as "beloved" or "soul of a car." Toyota's strategy continues to be a paradigm in today's world of multicultural marketing to connect consumers with brands and drive consumer purchase intent and sales across the world. It's no surprise that Toyota is one of the most loved brands in Japan.[27]

The automotive industry is certainly not short of examples as other automotive brands embrace the idea of connecting vehicles to human emotions too. Consider the collaboration between Buick (from Detroit's General Motors) and Oscar-winning actress and producer Reese Witherspoon's Hello Sunshine media company, which celebrates and empowers women by placing them at the center of every story. The "Dream with Us" brand campaign conveys an enhanced sense of well-being by focusing on the connection between vehicles and consumers.[28] It highlights Buick's future vision, "Imagining a world driven by technology that can see more, sense more, and connect more."[29,30] If you pay close attention to the word choices in this campaign, the effort to engage multiple senses becomes clear here, too. It seems the more senses you engage, the more memorable the experience and connection for your consumers, which is probably why brands are so focused on attaching human elements through marketing.

Ford's luxury vehicle division Lincoln invited Karriem Riggins, an American jazz drummer and hip hop producer, to remix alert tones for the all-new 2020 Lincoln Aviator, which were originally recorded by members of the Detroit Symphony Orchestra.[31] Listening to the commercial, emotions are referenced with the aim to inspire people through the music and driving.[32]

Our emotions are triggered when driving a car—whether it's a feeling of joy, safety, or an outburst of road rage—but our drives can also account for happy and memorable experiences. It's not a secret that the car-buying journey, and selling a car sometimes, can be emotional. The average person drives their car for a long time, so many factors and feelings come into play to enhance the interior atmosphere. Automotive companies understand what it means to humanize their brand and build positive relationships with consumers. When cars know how to sense people's emotions and react to them, they are personable and relatable in the eyes of the consumer. It doesn't even take a car enthusiast to connect in this special way.

Turning back time

Considering its first rebrand in 20 years, in 2021 the fast-food chain Burger King managed to engage consumers by building on nostalgia for its retro-inspired visual identity with a complete overhaul.[33] In a time where consumers are more health conscious and as a result, seek less processed and cleaner foods, it seems like Burger King decided to move toward a more realistic identity. In Chapter 4, I discussed Chobani's rebrand that was focused on a revised reconstruction of their brand image in the health food space. While Burger King was striving for a new identity, one that resembled real food, too, the rebrand was focused on bringing back positive times and memories with its retro-inspired look. It wasn't the only brand to invoke nostalgia with a rebrand or a campaign; the kids' meal throwback by McDonald's in 2022 was similar to this.[34] Targeting Millennials and Gen Z with a culturally relevant approach as a new way to appeal to customers seems to be part of the growth strategy.[35] This was done by taking one of the brand's most nostalgic experiences that was first introduced in 1979 and repackaging it in a relevant way for modern customers.[36] In the past, celebrity collaborations at McDonald's that included Saweetie, BTS, J Balvin, and Travis Scott were a big hit with younger audiences. This time around, by partnering with a streetwear brand, Cactus Plant Flea Market, who designed the toys and are known for celebrity collaborations, the effort proved to be a success, too.[37] But is the adult kids' meal really a nostalgia play if it targets adults this time around? Maybe. It could be strategic if you think about the fact that some people who grew up with this packaging have new or younger members of their family now. People will want to follow suit to relive old memories and share these with new family members or to replace memories, perhaps if they longed for this meal as a child.

The world's biggest build day with The LEGO Group

In 2020, the inaugural Brand Love Story report by Talkwalker identified The LEGO Group to be the most loved brand on social media after analyzing over 264 million conversations across social media, blogs, news, and forums, looking for phrases and mentions that indicate love and loyalty.[38] Besides focusing on the volume of positive mentions, several factors were measured such as the company's customer service, how the company practices corporate social responsibility, engagement, and feelings of nostalgia, among other factors.

Founded in 1932 by Ole Kirk Kristiansen, the brand is one of the leading toy manufacturers in the world[39] and excels in creating feelings of nostalgia, for instance with its *Friends* LEGO set. What's interesting, and probably not something you would expect, is that the brand strategically markets its products to adults (yup, to adults), growing its sales and profitability. For The LEGO Group, nostalgia starts with identifying adults as a key target audience, which has allowed the brand to diversify its product offerings across categories.

In conversation with The LEGO Group's Creative Director James Gregson, who oversees a team responsible for creating best-in-class product, brand advertising, and content, he shared some interesting insights with me. To him, "Nostalgia is not an overt marketing strategy but one that Millennials and Gen Z find incredibly compelling. Nostalgia brings back simpler times."[40]

Gregson explained that as sales soared, and meeting the new, heightened demand resulted in increased supply chain issues, The LEGO Group looked at ways to pivot their marketing communications from sales to engagement. With research showing that the holiday season is all about unwrapping gifts, typically followed by a drop in engagement immediately after the holidays are over, the brand wanted to continue engagement and traction in different ways. Inspired by Disney and Netflix who had created brand-owned cultural moments out of thin air, The LEGO Group team wanted to create its own.

The brand came up with a campaign to create LEGO Build Day, with its accompanying hashtag, #LEGOBuildDay, on December 27th, which included a slew of content to support those families building—everything from LEGO-built Yule log videos on YouTube to unboxing, sorting, and building tips. What started as a social media campaign scaled quickly to run in 13 different markets, including a TV ad in the U.K. on Christmas day, showing support from celebrities such as David Beckham, Chris Pratt, Orlando Bloom, and hundreds of thousands of fans from around the world.

Deemed a success, the campaign and marketing efforts were adopted and reignited the following year by the global department. It encourages people across the world to use their bricks and build something unique while sharing it with others by using the hashtag #LEGOBuildDay.

According to additional insights from The LEGO Group's Creative Director James Gregson, "The campaign isn't just about selling, it's about building."[41] During the pandemic, it was also about the responsibility to help families, so the brand flooded their channels with engagement-only content, live interviews, and build challenges, with the key focus around "Let's build together."

After all, creativity is a pure way of problem-solving and changing the narrative to deliver the message you want. Because even in a world that's highly digital, it goes back to the fundamentals that consumers appreciate, seeking tangible products and experiences to engage with brands. They fall in love as they create memories with families and friends.

Old memories that build connection

I remember when I was preparing for my speaking sessions across different cities in the U.S., I posted a question on social media asking what brands my connections loved and why. One of them stood out because it was different and unexpected. One person shared that she loves Tide, the laundry detergent brand by Procter & Gamble. For her, this detergent evokes an emotion and reminds her of her childhood. It's a brand who reminds her of her grandmother and in no way would she ever consider a substitute—regardless of other factors that could affect a consumer's decision such as price, quality, or customer service. It's hard to get people to switch from brands they've been accustomed to since their childhood. The social media post then sparked a memory from my past, when I used to visit the U.S. from Germany and stay at my grandparents' house as a child. I would always smell Clorox in the laundry room when entering the home through the garage. Or at my other grandparents' house when opening the fridge in the basement next to the pool table where I could always find a Vernors Ginger Ale in a green can with gold brand detailing. It never failed. Even the way the water smelled when taking a shower sometimes had an "American" scent. It was different than the water in Germany. I know, it sounds weird. To this day, I occasionally experience this different scent under the water and close my eyes to remember the days when I was a child visiting my family—summers that were filled with so much joy and happiness.

Meaningful memories like this stick with us and bring back feelings of warmth as we reminisce and recapture them as adults. Now that I live in the U.S., whenever I visit Germany, I have similar experiences. My sister and I usually save a small piece of luggage for foods and sweets, so we run off to the candy and chocolate aisle (yup, just like little kids haha) to see what we can bring back with us. While some are new products that may be exclusive to Germany or Europe, many are products that bring back childhood memories for us. Brands actively evoke emotions that encourage use and love for a brand.

Love Notes

1. **Use multisensory marketing**
   Use multisensory brand experiences to engage your consumers' senses holistically and create memorable experiences. Find natural ways to stimulate their senses, so you can create experiences in an omnichannel approach. The key is to engage multiple senses simultaneously.
2. **Consider olfactive branding**
   Sense and emotion work together to create memories. Think about how you can create or enhance the olfactive part of your brand to build powerful, emotional consumer connections that strengthen brand loyalty.
3. **Reveal your sound**
   What does your brand sound like? Embrace the power of sound by creating your own sonic identity that you can build on over time. Sound has an effect on behavior and can help you appeal to consumers' emotions if done right.
4. **Bring back happy times**
   Nostalgia entails sentimental longing for the past that brings about happy personal associations tied to a period or place. These feelings are typically personal and meaningful, and bringing these back through marketing initiatives can create deep and memorable connections with your customers.

PART THREE
Rational drivers

09 Relevance, differentiation, and consistency

We know brands take a very long time to build. After I started my own company in 2017, one of my mentors looked at me and said, "It will probably take you about three years to really be where you want to be with your brand." I looked at him, surprised. "Think about it," he said. "You have to establish a presence and name for yourself, gather consumer insights to understand how to adjust or better position your brand uniquely, and get comfortable with who your brand is and where it's going." This was one of the moments where I stopped for a minute to absorb everything he was telling me. There are moments in life that become more meaningful because you realize they only happen once. When I know I'm going to remember them forever, that's when I do a panoramic view of the room and take a mental video. Every so often I do this. From that moment on, I started paying close attention to how the brand continued to grow over the years.

Keep it relevant

As you operate a business or manage a brand, it's crucial to understand the importance of staying relevant and providing value nonstop. If you become irrelevant, you won't matter much to existing or potential customers.

In a conversation with one of my former marketing professors, Dr. Jeff Stoltman shared that, "Advertising can't overcome an inferior product. It doesn't compensate for the product being irrelevant. Good advertising has to be for a product that is performing." So, even with the right marketing or budget, you can't buy your customers' love for a product that can't seem to fit in their lives.

Many e-commerce giants cause brick-and-mortar businesses to become irrelevant after their rise. If we consider the rise of the internet and technology in general, the businesses that survive are prepared to grow into a new space. In a world where we can go online to find a date or order anything our heart desires, it's increasingly difficult to hold attention and maintain relevance. Brands are no different. The brands who are successful remain relevant *over* time and change *with* time. That's why flexibility with changes on the horizon and new trends is essential for long-term growth and success.

Focus on how people experience your brand

My mentor's timeline was accurate, to say the least. When Blended Collective hit that three-year mark, I thought back to what he'd said and thought to myself how spot-on he'd been. It took time to understand how our brand was perceived in the community and whether it aligned with the way we wanted to be perceived: authentic, cultural, and diverse. It took time to understand in what ways people experienced our brand, what our name meant to them, and how they identified with it. Our name reflects a "collective" of different cultures coming together, or the team we have in-house, in a way where we all "blend" or come together using our "collective" and individual identities. This reminds me of the classic book *The Prophet* by Lebanese American poet and writer Kahlil Gibran, in which he talks about the fundamentals of life. In the part about marriage, one of the fundamentals, Gibran says to "fill each other's cup but drink not from one cup."[1] It's a profound message that was published in 1923—one that reminds people that even when married and in togetherness, there should still be moments to foster individuality. Don't depend on each other for everything. That's a good lesson for consumers, too, as we experience strong connections with brands and feel like we're going through a divorce the minute our favorite product gets discontinued. Is there a healthy way to be attached to a brand without completely depending on it? It might be tough when brands can almost occupy the same space in a consumer's mind as our partners do when we consider them to be relevant.

People love referring to us as "Blended" for short. Most people outside of our company call us this, and it makes me feel like how I would refer to it in conversation, as if it were a child. "How's Blended?" is what I get asked sometimes. In fact, that's exactly what it feels like as a founder and business owner—as if my company is my child.

I remember early on when I decided to start the business, I said to myself, "If you're going to do this, you're going to commit to doing this forever." At the time, I thought it would have to be forever. I've stopped putting this pressure on myself and I'm aware that I don't have to run my business until the day I die.

Starting a business was so serious to me and I knew I would do everything in my control to make it work, to make it successful. I knew what it was like from past jobs where I invested the same type of passion and love for the work I was doing, but when you're not calling the shots or writing the checks at the end of the day, it's not the same. Working for someone, the risk wasn't mine to take, and I would still get paid no matter what. Though I like to think that failure is not an option for me, the reality is that entrepreneurs do fail. It's how you respond to and learn from failure that will set you apart. The passion, determination, and perseverance you decide to invest in your business will translate into your brand and how people experience it. Be mindful of the lasting impression you want others to have of your brand.

Redefine your brand assets

When I think about the ongoing learning moments that I've experienced in running a business, especially in the first few years, I realize how they allow my team and I to adjust and perfect the brand as needed to ensure that we can be relevant in the market, not just for the time being but for a long time to come. Visually, for example, our brand needed to be more functional after we launched. We didn't make this change until our first year in business because we used our brand design across various applications and settings that we couldn't test prior to launch.

Consumer insights are crucially important to perfect your positioning in the marketplace. We collected insights from clients but also heavily through our Speaker Event Series where people would come up and tell us how much they identified with the business name and how it resonated with them. We chose a slightly thicker font for functionality purposes while maintaining the juxtaposition of the upper-case "BLENDED" in a thin font and an all lower-case "collective" in a thicker font, both communicating a strong presence on their own but also very well together, kept in place by a thin vertical line that maintains the "togetherness" of the logo and visual design. Our design elements were updated with a subtle color change to display a more vibrant purple and while many wouldn't notice the difference, this minor change allows our brand to be more functional across the board. The color purple represents artistic and creative expression, intuition, originality, and the potential to reach a higher level. Using distinctive brand assets allows you to stand out in a unique way.

Create names with emotional appeal

The greatest brand names are the ones that evoke an emotion. My team and I apply the same creative naming process when we work on developing a brand for a new client—one that includes emotion. However, that's not all there is when it comes to naming a brand or even a product. For one of our projects in 2022, we started working with a new client as they were reconsidering a new name after being known as *Splendiferous Games* in the early stages of their business.[2] They are a game shop that fosters community and adventure in a fun and welcoming environment, and founders Aisha Blake and Benjamin Lippi want to build an inclusive community through gaming where people can feel safe. "We loved the original name, but too many people had trouble spelling or pronouncing it," Ben told me.[3] The original name was hard for the average gamer to pronounce and difficult to remember. It also didn't convey the right story and meaning that was embedded in the story of the founders, which they weren't sure how to communicate to the outside world when approaching us early on.

We worked with the founders to extract their core values and goals. This is one of my favorite things to do with a company who is receptive to it. The values of a company live, in most cases, within the founders. Sometimes they live within a whole team of people, though, like the brand or marketing team. Depending on who you work with and the type of brand, you might be able to find ways to let this mission-driven persona shine through. There are countless brands built based on who the founders are. And sometimes, customers see themselves in the founder or leader of a company. In collaboration with the client, we go on this long journey of research and brand exercises where even the founders will be surprised at what resides within them that we can help activate and bring to life in creative ways. And in this case, it revolved around finding a new business name—one that leaned into a feeling.

When working with clients, these are the questions we ask and actions we suggest as next steps to determine the right name:

1 Is it available?

- Availability spans from checking to see if social media handles and the domain are available. If you're considering protecting your name or business from the get-go, as you should, it's worth doing a trademark search early on before you decide on a name. Changing this down the road is costly and time-consuming, and entails having to create brand awareness all over again. Checking for name availability should always be done in the early stages of the naming process as unavailability will prompt you to consider other options.

2 Is it clear and user-friendly?

- Your brand name should be clear and straight to the point. It should be easy to identify, spell, pronounce and use. Sometimes using the founder's name can serve you well depending on the industry you're in. This might be more common for service professions such as doctors and attorneys but certainly is visible in other categories too, such as Jeni's Splendid Ice Creams.

3 Is it original?

- By researching your competitors in the industry, you can be sure to select a name that's different and unique to who you are. Being original makes you stand out and lets you occupy your own lane.

4 Is it memorable?

- Good names are easy to identify and remember. If your name doesn't resonate with people and is difficult to memorize, it might be tough to keep you top of mind in a crowded marketplace.

5 Is it culturally sensitive?

- Your name shouldn't have any negative connotations that might limit your brand from growing globally. It also shouldn't offend any cultural or marginalized groups, so it's important to conduct the right amount of research to avoid this and set yourself up for success from the start.

We strive to check the boxes for all these naming criteria throughout our process. I could go on and on about the process, but what's important here is the outcome. Utilizing our approach and naming process for our client, we eventually came up with compelling names that fit the founders, company, and what matters most to them. After hours spent on brand exercises and interviewing the founders, customers, and other partners, we landed on *Opal Grove Games*, a name that reflects both founders in a creative way and inspires conversation the moment you first hear it. The character Opal from the animated TV show *Steven Universe* sparked the motion for Aisha and Ben. In the show, the fusion form of Amethyst and Pearl together makes Opal. Amethyst and Pearl also happen to be the birthstones of the two company founders. With the combination of their core identities and inspiration from all of this serving as a metaphor for their relationship and what they're trying to build together, Opal Grove Games was born. Part of the name has a descriptive element, but the rest reflects the brand essence, that is the emotional brand experience or, as I like to call it, the heart and soul of the brand. This part is made up of a list of characteristics that describe the brand, such as being diverse, welcoming, adventurous, and surprising.

When searching for the right name, you want to avoid names that limit your brand, should the company expand into new categories down the road. You also want to stay away from names that have no meaning. Legally, it's also wise to avoid names that cannot be trademarked in your category. When I started my business, I quickly experienced that operating in the digital age has its downfalls and obstacles in relation to launching a new company and brand. The amount of work that goes into the name development, research, brand identity and strategy for a new company is an intense process and therefore should be enough motivation to determine the right timing to protect it early on. In my years of working with business owners and developing brands from scratch, I constantly come across businesses that spend thousands of dollars on brand assets with a name they don't bother to protect let alone check to see if it's available in their space. As a side note, you can have the same name as another business as long as you're both operating in a different category. Once your brand is created successfully, you continue to spend time perfecting all aspects of it—just like a home you maintain and update over the years to stay functional, safe, and current.

While your name doesn't have to be descriptive, it can be, and sometimes serves its purpose well if it's configured with online shoppers and SEO in mind. If you think about it, how common is it that a brand is used outside of its context, though? It's quite rare. An attractive name creates a premium, personal feel and should be fluent and easy to identify. People shouldn't be confused and wonder what it means. One name that comes to mind is LÄRABAR. The name promotes the product (energy bar) clearly as well as the founder's name. It's an interesting stylistic choice to go with all caps and the umlaut over the first vowel. Actually, until recently, I assumed that the "Ä" was pronounced the German way. After digging for an answer out of curiosity, I came across a Facebook post that lets people know that the umlaut is decorative.[4] I don't quite understand this choice, but I can respect it.

There are so many businesses across various industries who have created a strong name for themselves over time through brand association. They prove that you don't have to have a descriptive name to be successful and sometimes brands can even start out meaningless as long as they understand

and know how to attach emotion over time. It might be hard to believe that brands can launch with a name with no clear meaning, but if you take a look at existing brands and how they started out, it's possible. How? It could be as simple as the story that's attached to the name, the quality the brand is known for, or the short time it takes to say the name based on the rhythm or number of syllables, memorable cadences. Think back to a time before Apple… if not for them, would you ever associate the fruit with technology? Or electronics and Samsung before their launch? Brands like these are so embedded into our day-to-day lives that it might be tough to envision what life was like before them. They mark our life with a *before* them and *after* them. We make such strong brand associations with what they offer that their names almost directly correlate to the products or the industries they serve.

The most powerful brand names attract consumers and leave a long-term impression. Choosing a name that is unique and different is great, but also comes with a challenge to create a successful brand that has to be associated and paired with in the right way based on what you're in business for, which is usually easier to do with descriptive names. Great names communicate the brand identity and perhaps a descriptor phrase that communicates your *what*, a tagline that communicates your *how*, and your brand name rationale focusing on your *why*. From what I've seen, consumers place their focus on the *why* and *how* as much as on the *what* of the brand, which can be communicated by the name.

Sometimes you need to re-evaluate your brand and adapt to continue to be relevant. Being relevant means that you're delivering on a need your customers have and providing value to their lives. What you sell isn't always your value. It can be how you deliver it. All in all, it's not just about you—you have to find ways to make a difference. You're solving a problem in the marketplace and are offering a solution for your intended audience. As your customers evolve, your products and services should evolve to meet them where they are, too. When you sustain momentum in moments of turbulence, you create opportunities for both your customers and your brand to continue to grow together.

In the same way that brand relevance leads to strong and lasting connections between consumers and brands, striving to be different and unique helps you attain long-term success. Relevance and differentiation go hand in hand. To be relevant in a customer's or prospect's mind, there has to be something they recognize to be different about you. And when you're different, you still have to stay relevant.

Be different

With barriers to entry being low in the e-commerce space, it's as easy as ever to start a new business. But it's just as easy for competition to emerge. So many times, I've heard that business owners ought to create something that's better and different, not necessarily new. That is, they aren't trying to reinvent the wheel. There's nothing new; only new forms of delivery. When I think about the products and brands who are present in my day-to-day life, I can attest to this. Who invented the mobile phone? What was the first social media website? Who came up with the idea for rideshare? Who invented food delivery? I'm sure a number of brands you associate with doing these things popped into your mind just now, but it's important to recognize that these companies didn't invent anything. They just did it better than their competition. That's because you don't have to invent the industry you operate within, but you certainly do have to earn your place within it. Inventing a category or industry as one of the leaders can be expensive, but being a late early adopter like the companies who entered the spaces that I just mentioned may be the way to go. Why? Because you can learn from other companies' mistakes and failures as you prepare to enter the market.

Feel-good brands

Several years ago, I recall one of my cousin's obsession with LaCroix, an American carbonated, flavored water brand. She wasn't the only one. What seemed to be just sparkling water that promotes a sugar-free and healthier water became a cultural phenomenon. Though the colorful and distinct visual rebrand took years to explode after the product had been in the market for decades, it finally became part of mainstream culture around 2010.[5] The brand appeals to an entire demographic of Millennials and seems to position itself differently when you compare it to other brands who dominated the sparkling water space for decades and seem to appeal more to an older demographic. The latest on the scene at the time of writing is the super-hyped Liquid Death. This canned water resembles a can of beer and is mentioned on every social media outlet you can think of due to their distinct, over-the-top, and entertaining marketing that is everything but corporate. Packaging like this appeals to Gen Z, with an emphasis on heavy metal language.

What's interesting to me is the effective marketing strategies employed by so many water brands. You'd think water is water but clearly, it's not. At times, attractive brands catch fire, especially when they position themselves well on visual social media platforms like Instagram. When people gravitate toward a specific brand who reflects their values, particularly for Millennials and Gen Z, it makes them feel good. Younger generations are more inclined to show off the brands they use. They want to buy and support with a sense of pride. Consumers want to choose a brand who motivates them to be better in life and brings out the best version of them. It's not just about choosing the one you fall in love with but choosing the one that inspires you to be better every day. Just like the Orange Theory fitness studio I exercise at that has motivational quotes on the wall such as, "Good things come to those who sweat," or "Don't just wish for it, work for it." Brands who choose the indirect, soft sell approach and focus their efforts on shared brand values are some of the "feel-good brands" who build consumer-brand relationships slowly but surely; the ones who seem to make life better by being in it and being different.

Choosing a lane

Choosing to be and do different is one thing, but to communicate your competitive advantage or differentiating factors, you have to position your brand in the mind of the consumer accordingly. If your consumer or prospect can't tell that you're different, your strategy becomes irrelevant. Long story short, your brand differentiation has to be clear as day, which you can achieve by positioning your brand in the right way.

When I was an undergraduate student in college, I had to write a paper for my marketing class about analyzing different water brands and their brand positioning strategies. At the time, it was such an eye-opening assignment because I had not paid much attention to what seemed to be a boring product. Since then, I've not stopped paying attention to water brands and recently even mentioned it as an example when I was a guest speaker in a marketing class at a university. The professor had placed a bottle of FIJI Water on my podium right before I started speaking, so I referenced the brand to explain the importance of how we choose to position the brands we work for (or own), with an analogy of how we choose to position and present ourselves as personal brands, too. I looked at the class and said, "What is the difference between this FIJI Water bottle and all the others you see on your tables?" The undergraduate marketing students looked at me with anticipation to see what would follow next. "What are the values you associate with this water brand?" I asked. "Expensive, high-end, fancy, and premium," they started to share. I said, "These brand attributes you're sharing reflect the packaging and brand identity you've come to know over time. If I were to pour two different types of water into a cup without revealing the brand and ask you again what the difference is, the answers might be slightly different. You might not be able to tell."

I mean, I don't agree with the statement people make that all water tastes the same. Sometimes they go as far as saying all bottled water tastes like tap water, but here, too, I don't agree. Many of the water brands associate and differentiate their value with the source of where their water comes from, such as FIJI Water from the Fiji Islands or evian spring water from France. So, the more exotic or natural the location, the more expensive the water? Maybe, maybe not. Regardless of how premium the price, brand, taste, or hip the marketing, water is one of those products that we will always have to consume no matter what. In the same way, these branding strategies don't seem to be going away anytime soon.

Products may be similar on the surface, as we see with water brands, but how you communicate your values and position yourself as a brand is entirely original to each company. It also depends on the space you want to occupy in the market. As a result, you attract the group of people you want to reach repeatedly. The right branding and positioning can make all the difference when you're competing against other brands and products in the same category.

Less is more... sometimes

When you clearly differentiate your brand, you understand that you can't be everything to everyone. Focus is the way to go. Instead of trying to do it all, establish where your business can provide the best and most value that simultaneously allows you to meet consumer demands. Once you pair these two, focus on how you can be different.

In-N-Out Burger on the U.S. West Coast, for example, has a clear and concise menu with about five items on the list. You don't have to think twice about what to order. It might be a small product offering but it doesn't seem to diminish the success of the fast-food chain. To me, this is a good example of focusing on quality over quantity. When your product offering is so clear, you attract exactly who your brand is meant for—the right customer.

Still, less is only more in some cases. In 2016, when I was getting ready to move back home to the U.S. after spending a couple of years in Germany for graduate school, I was packing my luggage the night before my return flight. One of my friends was watching me trying to squeeze in everything I had accumulated over my nearly two-year stay, including last-minute chocolate and beauty purchases that wouldn't be available to me when I returned to the U.S. And suddenly, there they were... several bottles of the brand 8x4, the deodorant spray. "What in the world, Lydia? Why are you packing deodorants?" she asked. I giggled and explained that I wouldn't be able to find these in the U.S. because the market hadn't discovered them. So you understand, in the U.S. market at the time, deodorant roll-ons were more ubiquitous compared to spray bottles. Her reaction showed disbelief. She was shocked that Americans could be so behind. I know this sounds funny because the country that is known for "bigger is better," modern America that is, where my European friends tend to make fun of one-gallon shampoo bottles and larger-than-life toothpaste tubes, doesn't have a variety of deodorant options? Seriously? At the time, that was the situation indeed. I'm never overwhelmed when standing in the deodorant aisle trying to make a choice to buy because there aren't many options to begin with, unlike moments when I'm trying to find a bottle of shampoo where I'm faced with endless options. By the way, a few years later, this same friend of mine moved to New York to work at an ad agency. What was she responsible for? Overseeing and expanding the deodorant category.

Sometimes, consumers are more satisfied when they have options. I'm not talking about an overwhelming number of options, but a healthy number they can choose from to meet their needs—just like the choices we have as consumers when it comes to water. If these options are unique to the brand or category, all the better.

The premium ice cream brand Häagen-Dazs is a good example of using flavor uniqueness as a product differentiator across some of their assortment such as my go-to "white chocolate raspberry truffle" or "pineapple coconut." Or take the vegan creamery I consulted that is opening a shop that differentiates its brand by offering more options to vegan consumers that are currently not present in the region.

From different features, pricing strategies, or ingredients, the differentiation strategy is a way of brand positioning that matters. It encourages consumers to choose your brand over a competitor's. Being different doesn't always mean that you're unique but being unique or special certainly requires you to be different. A brand who indicates it's the same as other ones and not that different isn't likely to flourish; you can foresee it's not going to take off the way you wish it would. In the moment where consumers feel like you're the sole option to fulfill their needs and wants, they choose you. This is where you continue to move up the ladder of "The Eight Brand Love

Stages" to the level of attachment, love, and even loyalty. The rational drivers of being relevant and different, especially in this combination, signal to consumers that they're receiving the value they're paying for.

Consistency is key

Have you ever wondered why fast food tastes the same wherever you go around the world? Many chain restaurants put a strong emphasis on delivering consistent food and taste experiences for a reason. People I know who travel all over, resort to such fast-food chains as a backup whenever they don't like the local food. I remember when my sister, friend, and I spent time in Barcelona; they desperately wanted to escape all the seafood that they couldn't seem to get away from no matter where we decided to go for new food experiences. Burger King was their relief the minute they found one. This is not to say that global fast-food chains don't offer localized products or customization to some of their menu items because they definitely do. Like the McShrimp at McDonald's I saw in an ad when I was in Japan, or other product adaptations based on local ingredients, such as the Iced Date Macchiato at Starbucks or the McDonald's Chicken Big Mac during my time in Dubai. Products are locally adapted to suit people in that market based on preferences and consumer behavior. So yes, sometimes certain ingredients are substituted so you end up with barbecue sauce instead of mayonnaise on your sandwich. While surprise elements like this can disrupt a consumer's experience and make it less pleasant, the overall food experience across global chains is quite consistent.

It's safe to say consumers like to go back to places that provide great and consistent experiences. Consistency means stability and comfort.

Costco members enter the store with an expectation that they will save on products with bulk purchases and gas. As consumers, we like to know what to expect and to be aware of the value we will receive. Brand predictability is good in this way. As an Apple user, I know that I can sync everything across my devices whether it's the many color-coded calendars, the notes app on my phone that I pull up when I'm on my MacBook, or the nights I'm texting from my laptop because I left my phone in the other room. It's both consistent and convenient. When you are consistent as a brand, you strengthen the value of your product or service to consumers while earning credibility for delivering on your brand promise. But consistency doesn't end there.

Building value in your brand ecosystem

When building or growing your brand, be sure to create consistent experiences in more than just one way. Your customers should feel like they're in the same brand ecosystem across all touchpoints and interconnected channels, every single time they interact with your brand both online and offline. This includes the moment they step foot into your physical space, visit your website, go to your social media pages, receive an email, or complete a purchase. Depending on the type of business you have or industry you operate in, these customer touchpoints are different. When you're able to build such a consistent experience from start to finish, it helps you shape a consistent image and perception in your consumer's mind. Wherever, whenever, and however they experience you, they should be overtaken with a great experience every time.

The key is to focus on what you can nurture and where you can grow. What this means is that you don't have to be present on all social media platforms to be consistent but rather be strategic and selective. I've hosted many marketing workshops over the years and a regular question I receive is, "Do I have to be on all social media channels to succeed?" My answer is usually the same: no, you don't.

When you understand who your target audience is and where they spend their time, such as the platforms they use, you can be right where they're looking. You want to be accessible as this is a great way to engage current customers while also searching for prospects. Social media can be really time-consuming when you're present everywhere; you risk spreading yourself too thin. Instead, focus on platforms and content mediums where you feel comfortable creating content and building an active presence. Quality over quantity. Consistency over quantity.

The goal is to position yourself to be remembered and trusted. These positive feelings toward your brand can earn you plenty of loyalty points. It might be easier said than done to establish a consistent brand because the truth is that it can be challenging to be consistent time and time again. Consistency is about repetition. When you know what works well based on customer feedback, you strive to repeat it but also should have an open mind to becoming and doing better. We do the same thing in our personal lives, don't we? When we don't get a good result from our actions, we're told to try different actions to see new results. When we know something yields a positive result, we repeat it. It's no different with brands who are consistent; they resonate on a higher level and deliver the right value.

Establishing brand architecture for consistency

With distribution in premier grocery markets, Blended Collective client Fusion Epicure offers healthy snack choices by using authentic ingredients in the form they were created, without human processing.[6] Made from natural ingredients, the brand delivers distinct quality, flavor, and nutrition. As the brand looked to the next stage of growth in 2019, they required a brand architecture strategy for the evolving brand portfolio, including the popular Sesame Squared and fine European chocolate products.[7] The challenges were obvious—how to strategize the corporate brand and product brands in the brand portfolio that have the same name and are difficult to distinguish when expanding into new, multicultural target groups, markets, or categories.[8]

The process of brand architecture helps you stay organized with your in-house portfolio while making the relationship between all your brands or products clear to consumers, sending the right communication to enable the perception you want them to have. Brand architecture helps you see how and at what level brands are connected to each other. It's a tool to identify a brand structure. And sometimes, a company may choose not to connect the two for a strategic reason.

Think about Procter & Gamble, or P&G, the consumer goods company. P&G serves as a good example of brands who are housed under this one holding company, yet when browsing through their portfolio, none of the brands have a clear connection to their parent brand. It's safe to assume that this is done intentionally as each brand encompasses its own brand identity and attributes, targeting different demographics with different values to the point where people rarely associate P&G with brands across different categories and diverse products like Oral-B (oral care), Pampers (baby care), or Tide (fabric care). Doing it in this way requires an extensive budget, as you can imagine. You're essentially developing a house of individual brands who operate completely independent of the parent brand. Everything you develop for one brand, you have to develop for the other as there is no connection between any of them as well as no primary model you're following per se. Additional work can involve anything from new messaging to websites.

On the other hand, you have brands like FedEx who associate their brand name with all of their brand offerings like FedEx Ground, FedEx Freight, or FedEx office. This strategy encourages consumer purchases and value based on the strong brand recognition and name that both exist. The main brand theme or elements are typically reflected throughout the other brands, which is a more affordable and simpler strategy. You also work on developing one strong brand that can carry through the rest of your portfolio well. Over time, this also helps build strong brand equity. In either instance, there is logic and strategy attached when a company decides to sell different products under different brand names.

A third option is to have a more affordable and flexible brand structure—that is a hybrid of these two models like Marriott does with JW Marriott and Sheraton hotels. In this case, brands can choose when to associate with the parent brand based on their marketing goals. I can go on about brand architecture with examples like Coca-Cola in many different verticals, Ford, or Volkswagen, which includes notable German and Italian brands in the portfolio of vehicles. There are different ways to organize and structure your brands, and which one you choose depends on the goals you want to achieve for all of your brands in the long run.

In auditing the Fusion Epicure brand, evaluating the brand architecture and positioning, I made recommendations to increase clarity, efficiency, and consistency to avoid consumer confusion in the marketplace.[9] To create strong brand awareness and better leverage the master brand, the most recognizable of all brands, it's linked to all product brand names, yet making the individual brands, or sub brands, more distinct by adding new product names to fit into their respective categories.[10] Fusion Epicure is positioned to be consistent with their brand names across all platforms to have meaning beyond a healthy snack. With a coherent brand architecture in place, this makes it easy for target customers to find the right product and differentiate between brand offerings in the market as brand recognition is reinforced consistently.[11]

Whether you choose a house of brands like P&G, a branded house like FedEx, or a hybrid of the two brand architecture models, either strategy is a way for you to clearly position your brand and value proposition in the market. Based on the audiences you want to reach, you can cross-promote and sell across your different brands and products.

To raise the game as a brand leader, determine how your brand can be relevant to the market you intend to serve. The more relevant your brand is, the less you have to worry about competitors because customers perceive you as relevant in their overwhelming number of choices. While being relevant is a strong foundation for any brand, so is being different to avoid being the same as everyone else in the market. Finally, consistency is key, too, when customers interact with you. They want to know what they can expect from you every single time and feel comfortable and stable in this consumer-brand connection.

Love Notes

1 **Stay relevant**
When you stay connected to your current and potential customers to understand what they're looking for, you can deliver products and services that are relevant to their lives. Stay relevant so they'll want to keep you around.

2 **Stand out in a crowded market**
By being different, you position yourself to stand out in a crowded marketplace. In your consumer's mind, you want to be perceived in a distinctive way compared to your competitors or why else would they choose you? Strive to be different and unique, such as by using distinctive brand assets that set you apart.

3 **Choose a name that goes a long way**
Find a name that reflects who you are and can grow with you. Your name should be clear, original, memorable, and culturally sensitive. Above all, it has to be available. Make sure to protect it early on, so you don't have to build your brand assets and recognition again from scratch.

4 **Be consistent across the board**
When you create consistency in your offerings, your customers know what to expect from you. They want to know the value they're going to receive by interacting with your brand. Know what works well and continue to repeat these valuable actions while also keeping an open mind and open heart for improvements.

10 Experience, innovation, and convenience

Choice can overwhelm consumers. As shown in Chapters 4 and 9, differentiation and relevance can really impact the consumer in a positive way if done right. If done poorly, well…

An example of this is best characterized by an experience I had during the home remodeling process when I was in the market to buy a new toilet. I began to ask myself question after question. Going into this search, the only thing I knew I wanted to look for was soft-close hinges for the seat. Everything else was up in the air. The second I started looking, I was overwhelmed. Do I want a round or oval toilet seat? What size? There are different sizes? What's the size of the rough? What about the height of the toilet? Standard or comfort height? Oh, and don't forget about the GPF (gallons per flush). I made it far enough in to even start looking at flush handles. Seriously. I remember my friend saying, "Are you kidding? It's just a toilet." It might just be a toilet, but when you pick one, you don't want it to become a pain in the you know what after it's installed. And with a shortage in supply and backorders, I knew I didn't want to wait too long either. The entire process was so overwhelming until I finally decided which toilets to buy after hours and hours of research and reading online reviews. When customers are faced with obstacles such as buying some new piece of furniture or amenity for the first time, brands should try to help their target audience through the experience. This experience shouldn't be complicated or busy—it should be simple and straightforward. The right brands make our lives easier.

When customer service matters

I spent the same amount of time researching most items during the home remodeling process as I had done trying to find the perfect toilet. With some products and services, my frustration grew. It was mostly related to the customer service experiences I had with different stores and brands over months.

It seems like 2022 was the year of bad customer service. At least for me. It made me appreciate the brands who offer positive customer experiences, as it feels important to matter when you're in the middle of a stressful shopping experience. And for quality customer service, I'm willing to spend top dollar.

Customer service and customer experience go hand in hand with brand love. How can we ever "love" a brand that cultivates a negative customer experience? It's part of the whole package. It seems more challenging to come across good businesses who care and go the extra mile post-pandemic, so much so that when companies do this, they stand out. I'm aware that more people write reviews after an emotional experience, positive or negative. Brands have a responsibility to provide positive experiences for customers, though. While customers don't want employees to go beyond their job descriptions, they should be able to seek human decency from a brand. As someone who sees this as incredibly important, I like to write positive reviews for brands I interact with as much as possible.

During the same remodel, I also had to figure out AVAC and HVAC systems. I had an experience with an air duct cleaning company that was the best I've had in a long time. Customer service is relevant in all places without a doubt, but who would think it would be with an air duct cleaning company? After finding the information through a quick online search and finding few reviews, I called the company for a quote. I was then walked through the process from beginning to end, which immediately made me feel comfortable because I knew what to expect, setting my expectations high from the start. To confirm my service appointment, I received an email and as it got closer to the date, received reminder calls as well. It wasn't too much though—it was just enough communication, the right communication. When the service day came, the crew was running a little behind, and a service representative called, explained, apologized, and offered a discount to compensate for the upcoming expected delay. I was so well taken care of by that call that I forgot they were even running late. The heads up gave me notice that was useful, and I appreciated it. The service ended up being great and was followed by a call asking about my experience this time. The value I received was unmatched by any service I had received in a while. When they asked about my experience, I was happy to explain what I enjoyed about it. I was also pleased to get to speak with a live person rather than a computer. I wanted to be sure to let them know how much I appreciated their level of communication and attention to detail. Exemplary customer service of this kind stands out, especially in stressful circumstances. A satisfied customer cares about receiving the right quality considering the price they pay. They want value. Whenever they feel like they're getting value for their money, they're less likely to complain, more likely to return for repeat purchases even at a higher price, and eventually refer you to others without having to think twice.

This is the ultimate stage you want to reach in the "The Eight Brand Love Stages" because it results in loyalty and advocacy for the brand. Delivering on multiple drivers, both emotional and rational throughout the customer journey, is key to get to this stage.

The customer is always right

At Blended Collective, we also put an emphasis on customer experience and customer service. Our process is a bit different than what companies coming to us implement for standard consumers. But it's not truly different. We want to know what we do well and what we don't because the reality is, it's the only way to become better. How else would you know how you're performing? Measuring customer feedback is important, and you can do this by calculating a Net Promoter Score, also known as NPS, a metric that presents one question to measure the likelihood of a customer recommending your company to another person, identifying promoters and detractors.

Gathering customer feedback allows you to make improvements as needed to positively affect brand loyalty and revenue in the long run. In short, the customer experience matters. In the U.S., the motto "the customer is king" or "the customer is always right" is embedded into our minds to remind us that the customer dictates our business. I mean, it's true because what business do you have without your customers to begin with? But in other cultures and countries, in Germany, for example, when the customer is wrong, a business will certainly let them know. I've experienced it one too many times. If a sales associate doesn't agree with you, they will not budge. And the best part is… they don't care if you leave and never come back. Yup! Having lived in the U.S. for most of my adult life, I experience a culture shock every time I go back to Germany to visit because I'm so spoiled with the customer service in the U.S. where in the end, it's always about making a customer happy when doing business with them. In Germany, not so much.

Customer experience is a relevant rational driver in the consumer-brand journey but can certainly be emotional too. It's important to consider both emotional and rational (or functional) drivers to optimize the customer experience as consumer needs constantly shift and evolve. By seeking a harmonic balance between the two driver categories, emotional connections can be strengthened on the path to brand love.

Walking the line between function and emotion

Brands such as Kodak, known for their photo film business, and Nokia, a global phone brand, are classic examples that continue to be referenced as brands who didn't innovate with changing technology to re-position in time, as their vulnerability to competitive forces ultimately led to brand failure. They simply didn't change fast enough. Innovations can fail for various reasons such as a lack of customer research to ensure a market for the intended innovation, poor forecasting, missed features, a complex product, and weak distribution support, among many other reasons. Yet, there are countless innovations that have taken the market by storm. A notable one is the Beautyblender, an egg-shaped make-up sponge that changed the beauty game. Make-up sponges existed long before this came to life but clearly not in the same way. You rarely see a beauty tutorial on YouTube or a make-up artist where the Beautyblender is absent, even if it is a knockoff of the popular brand.

Products that make such an impact in a category modernize the world and enhance business. They don't have to be complex. In fact, they can be very simple and still play a tremendous role, as well as change how we go about our day-to-day lives. The right product can have an immediate impact in your life and make you wonder, "How did I live without this all of these years?" That's what I thought when I discovered an umbrella locker to avoid creating puddles indoors during my visit to a restaurant in Japan. Let me tell you… the umbrella culture in Japan is as serious as it sounds.

Brands need to be remarkable. They shine when they make an impact on the consumer. One way to do this is by creating something new and unexpected that consumers didn't know they needed. The Beautyblender was innovative, just like Apple is and continues to be. They didn't invent the computer. They just reinvented it. Innovation comes from looking outside of your category and taking it back to the drawing board to find ways to integrate this into your product or experience.

When I work with brands, I encourage them to do this very same thing: to look beyond their own industry. When you learn about the successes and failures of others, you can fine-tune the path for your own business in a way that works for you. This is where most of the learning and growth happens. Looking inside of your industry is a no-brainer, but as a clothing brand, for instance, what can you learn from the automotive industry?

As brand marketers, remember to look outside of your industry for inspiration. To stimulate creativity, you should constantly consume external content. Read new books, listen to new podcasts, meet new people, and have new experiences. These external opportunities drive innovation, which doesn't have to start with products. Innovation can start with people, too.

How Warby Parker innovates and disrupts the eyewear market

Warby Parker is an excellent example of an innovative brand focused on people. At a $95 starting price, I personally felt like I hit the jackpot with a new pair of high-quality glasses plus free shipping and return. There has been much buzz and hype around Warby Parker since the brand was founded in 2010, so much so that I wanted to experience it for myself. As someone who was buying and wearing eyewear for fashion purposes for years, part of me was secretly excited when I was finally told I needed glasses with a minor prescription. A reason to buy even more eyewear! I'm particular with glasses that fit my facial features, so I made some time to stop by the Warby Parker store in Chicago while I was visiting my sister after I received my prescription. This is one of the brand experiences I was intentional about having as a consumer. I wanted to experience it both online and offline to see what the hype was about.

Warby Parker launched as an innovator of the DTC model. Before they came onto the scene, buying eyewear was not as much of an experience for consumers. The only time I personally experienced eyewear as a social experience was when I was in Amsterdam. My friend and I sought out vintage eyewear showrooms that offered deadstock, inventory that never sold from previous decades but that also wasn't produced anymore. These showrooms are usually quiet spaces that you can book by appointment only. They make you feel special, knowing that not everyone has what you're about to buy. And whether you want to or not, these eyewear pieces you buy are somehow always conversation starters. It never fails. It didn't take long until I was asked by someone who passed me on the street (after buying a new pair and wearing them immediately) if she could borrow my glasses for a photoshoot right then and there. And in a similar way, my eyeglasses from Warby Parker spark the same connection with people though they're not vintage, deadstock, or rare in the sense that nobody is wearing a similar style. If anything, it's the opposite. People connect with me because they recognize the brand or might have the same pair. "Oh, are those Warby Parker? I have the same exact style." Or "that's the one I want to buy next." Because of the low price point, it's not rare for people to have multiple frames to switch up their style whenever they feel like it.

Consumers can bond over similar taste and preferences. When I see someone who wears or uses the same thing as me, in a way, it indicates that they're speaking my language. It makes me wonder if there's more to the person that might align with the way I live my life. Maybe a bond that's worth exploring further? Great brands create connections between consumers and the brand, but the best brands seem to connect consumers with other people. This is how connections and positive experiences happen that, in turn, inspire positive consumer-brand moments.

From DTC startup to big retail

Digital-first brands have the benefit of tapping into their consumers directly by avoiding the middleman. When creating a prototype product, they can gather first-party data and immediate feedback from their consumers and use it as input to perfect their final products. Digital touchpoints can create strong personal bonds long before the physical experience with the product takes place, especially for Millennials and Gen Z. The digital-first connection doesn't end digitally though. With beauty apps offering tools to virtually try on make-up, you can use your phone's camera to explore what make-up will look like on your face before making a purchase. Technology like this continues to appeal to end-users who are looking for direct ways to engage and buy from a brand. It's exciting to see what brands can do when they connect with consumers in this way. NYX, the color cosmetics brand, is credited as a "digital first" brand who considered social media initiatives before it was the thing to do, attracting and reaching younger consumers in the early 2000s[1] before being acquired by L'Oréal in 2014 for a reported $500 million.[2] For a brand with humble beginnings, this is an impressive milestone to reach.

In similar ways, with Warby Parker starting out as a DTC brand but also operating from 200 brick-and-mortar locations as of 2022,[3] the brand seems to be doing well with an innovative business model that continues to disrupt the eyewear market. The retail stores appear to feed the consumer need to socialize in a way that's different and innovative. When was it fun to go to the store and try on prescription glasses before? By opening retail stores and scaling the brand, Warby Parker is also able to offer services that would be difficult online: eye exams. By doing so, the company is offering a more holistic experience to consumers and further eliminating the need to go anywhere else throughout the consumer journey to find the right pair of glasses. On the other hand, their digital presence seems to be satisfying consumers who are looking for convenience while shopping, too. By allowing you to try on five frames in the comfort of your home with free shipping and returns, it operates with a key priority in mind for e-commerce growth to attract and retain new customers. The customer journey at the Warby Parker store began with me being warmly greeted and assisted from the start until I found a pair that suited me. I was probably in the store for almost two hours, trying on different styles and thinking to myself, "They're going to tell me to stop trying on glasses any moment now." They didn't. They were there all along, handing me pair after pair with a smile. Upon finally making a purchase and providing my email address to sign up for their newsletter, I continued to engage with the brand on social media. The seamless integration of digital and physical efforts through omnichannel retailing is truly what appears to set them apart—from email reminders about another pair I had tried on in the store but didn't purchase, to emails inquiring about my experience both during and post purchase. After all, the brand went from online to retail because it was so consumer-driven.[4] The retail experience clearly enhances the positive customer experience altogether. Social media posts shared on Warby Parker's platforms include powerful, emotional language about how good customers feel after engaging with the brand.

When you create happy customers who become your cheerleaders, you leave them feeling good about themselves and your brand. It's a fine line you're tapping into between delivering on functional needs through your products, such as eyewear, and creating emotional bonds through meaningful experiences, both in person and on social, that leave your customers yearning for more.

Connect your values to your story

It wasn't until my eyewear arrived in the mail (the color of the style I wanted wasn't available at the store), that I came across the 100-word story printed on the lens cloth labeled "Warby Parker in 100 Words"[5] about how the brand started. I'm reminded of the story every time I clean my glasses. Before that though, when opening the case, I'm greeted with a short message that reads "Nice to see you."[6] These are additional features of why the brand is so cool and resonates with people. I can't remember a time I celebrated a cleaning cloth for any pair of eyewear I bought. Yes, even the expensive, designer vintage pairs.

The conversation with the Warby Parker brand continued beyond the store experience, beyond the website, beyond the emails. It continued right here in my living room as I was cleaning my glasses. I catch myself reading it every now and then—it's so short and sweet. It's inspiring because it tells the story of the brand's WHY, the reason it was born into the world of eyewear. It basically revolves around the gap in the industry for providing an affordable pair of vision and prescription glasses that are usually known to be quite expensive once it's all said and done. Prescription eyeglasses don't have to be expensive and style doesn't have to be either. The brand does a wonderful job of reminding you of this throughout all consumer touchpoints. The story remains consistent wherever you go. The pain point people experience is expensive glasses and Warby Parker provides the solution by offering affordable glasses alongside a holistic experience. Part of their story is that they want to "inspire and impact the world with vision, purpose, and style—without charging a premium for it."[7] With a lower price point as one way the brand seems to position itself as different, Warby Parker provides additional value through convenient ways of shopping with their Home Try-On program and a socially engaging experience that has innovatively changed the way people purchase eyeglasses altogether.

Balancing price and convenience while providing products with plenty of options seems to work well for brands who want to monetize convenience in a clever way to attract and retain consumers. Still, there are many more lessons you can take away from a brand like Warby Parker. The brand is a reminder that even when you're focused on providing such functional or rational benefits in your industry, emotion is still an important element to consider. Here, it's by sharing your story anytime, anywhere. Consumers care to know the story behind your brand because many times, connections between brands and people are built through stories that are shared. When you're consistent with your story by also including your key value or benefit that meets consumer needs, it makes everything come together. Adhering to your core values communicates a serious effort on your part and allows you to stick to your brand strategy and authentic brand voice.

The convenience culture

As much as we as humans are creatures of habit, I believe we are also creatures of convenience. Consumers are addicted to convenience. They trade money for convenience. The success of Amazon is proof of this.

When looking for convenience, consumers have to decide where they want to spend their money. In a world of millions of product options to choose from, consumers are looking for better and faster ways to get their hands on the products and services they desire. The easier it is to engage with your business and get what they're looking for when and where they need it, the happier they'll be. While convenience many times comes with a cost, it typically results in saving time and energy that can be spent in other meaningful ways. Besides, who doesn't want their customers to stick around? The brands who know how to provide convenient options in the right way are the ones who are high on the list of consideration for a consumer who is willing to pay. Whether it's a faster checkout process, the ability to order online (especially on their smartphones), or loyalty reward programs, what keeps consumers coming back is a convenient way to meet their needs on their own terms they continue to define.

Driving through the "fast" lane

In the early days after moving to the U.S., I found myself living in a state of surprise. In Europe, the only drive-thru we grew up with was the one that had the big "M" and eventually Burger King at select locations. Oh, and of course a car wash. Even today, at least based on my latest visit to Germany, I'm not familiar with any other drive-thrus that exist there. I wonder if this level of innovation will ever make it to Europe. So, when I discovered pharmacy and bank drive-thrus in the U.S., it was a foreign business concept to me that conveyed laziness. I don't know why but at the time, I didn't connect it with the value of convenience. What was so difficult about getting out of your car and walking into a pharmacy or bank for five minutes to take care of business? I felt so strongly about this that it took me seven years to even give it a try. Guess what? Since then, I don't walk into a pharmacy or bank unless I absolutely have to. Go figure! Isn't that how it goes? You never know unless you try.

Drive-thrus are all about convenience and effectiveness; you don't have to park and get out of your car to go inside. That is, in normal times when we're not faced with the after-effects of the COVID-19 pandemic that continues to cause labor shortages, increasing our wait times in drive-thrus.[8] Nevertheless, they did provide comfort and safety for many people during these challenging times when they generally felt less safe inside restaurants or buildings, which were closed in some cases. As I've already shared, convenience is associated with value. So, when it's not delivered in the way customers are expecting, customer satisfaction drops. The number of times I decided to leave a drive-thru lane that I was waiting in this year alone supersedes the number of times I've done that in my entire life. I'm not kidding. Drive-thrus are, in fact, slower and less accurate compared to what customers are used to.[9] To continue to deliver a competitive advantage and ensure businesses are thriving, meeting customer expectations, even in a drive-thru, is key. When people lose the very same thing they come to you for, convenience in this case, it's easier for them to abandon you and seek a new path.

Why convenience matters

In October 2022, I attended an annual fundraising event that had been hosted virtually for the previous two years. It was really exciting to get to see everyone after such a long period of isolation and so many virtual meetings with many of these same individuals. Social media was proof of that the following day. My friend messaged me on Instagram and said, "How was the event? I had FOMO." FOMO is the "fear of missing out," and it's a perception that we develop based on content we see on social media. We feel like we're "missing out" when we keep up with social happenings online rather than in person. Thanks to the internet, people are more likely to experience such feelings that can spark all sorts of emotions—both good and bad. For consumers, the desire to keep up and satisfy their need for instant gratification is only growing with the internet.

These days, it's easy to obtain what we want and when we want it to satisfy that immediate desire. It's the consistent chase for satisfaction and happiness to occur as quickly as possible. It can't happen fast enough. For some, it's the number of likes on social media as soon as they make a post and for others it's a pizza arriving at the door in a matter of minutes thanks to food delivery apps. Or what about companies who offer same-day delivery?

Subscription services we can sign up for like Amazon Prime fulfill the need for constant gratification, also allowing consumers to skip advertising with a simple click of a button to upgrade to premium. Convenience and speed at its finest. In times like this where I catch myself being a victim by demanding such a high level of convenience, I try to self-control and tell myself that I can and should be patient. What's another day? Sometimes that's easier said than done though. Consumers have become accustomed to a certain standard when interacting with brands and don't want to settle for anything less. At times, it feels like the values people hold, such as supporting small businesses by buying local and not supporting corporate giants, go out the window quickly. "It's too convenient for me to care," is something I've heard from people in my network. People don't like delayed gratification though the reality of what they have to deal with in times of supply chain issues looks a lot different.

When consumers were left with nothing but months of wait time for products that they took for granted until they were faced with the COVID-19 pandemic and real consequences, their day-to-day lives were affected in every aspect you can imagine. Regardless, as consumers, we want what we want and when we want it. Convenient products make our lives easier and save us time; and time is money that can be invested elsewhere.

Loyalty that lasts

The best bank promotions can earn you over $600 just for switching your bank and setting up a new account. Yes, I know, these offers typically come with a list of requirements you have to meet but the minute you do, you've earned yourself some nice cash. Even with such offers though, a loyal customer will not be swayed. This is the difference between transactional business and a customer who is loyal. For them, cash simply isn't enticing enough because they choose your brand for more than that—for the right reason. If you have both iPhone and Android users in your network, you know exactly what I'm talking about. The battle for customer loyalty between the two is real. No matter what side, both users seem to be so convinced of their choice and clear as to why they don't care to switch. That is, unless you give them a reason to make the move.

To go beyond being a transactional brand and keep your customers coming back, brands create loyalty programs that are meant to provide benefits and perks. More than that, they focus on building an emotional relationship throughout the buyer's journey that differentiates their position in your eyes. Emotions in relationships are key. And brands can build relationships with humans in the same way. The higher the level of emotional attachment, the higher the dependency on the brand. If you inspire emotional connection, people will get behind you and show you loyal behavior more than ever. But how do you incentivize the behavior you want them to adopt, so they can truly turn into loyal customers? Some of it starts with an innovative loyalty program that provides a valuable, personal experience time and time again.

The right rewards create loyalty

It's probably safe to say that people will change their behavior for a good loyalty program. Think about those who swing by Starbucks to redeem their complimentary birthday reward or use Chipotle's loyalty rewards program that unlocks free guacamole. It's clear that a completely different level of value is provided to the customer throughout their shopping experience. For some companies it's easier than others. Whereas grocery and retail stores offer endless ways to connect with their customers through their reward programs, the stores that focus on using coupons regularly to get people in the door are devaluing their offerings to the point where customers are no longer willing to pay regular price. They'll go purchase somewhere else the moment they don't have access to your coupons any longer. Besides this, customers place importance on understanding what a loyalty program is going to demand of them, too. Is it simple to use? Do they have to download an app? Is there a need to carry a physical card? Do they have to give away too much personal data?

To create valuable and innovative reward programs, companies have to collect, analyze, and understand their customer data. I remember several years back when I was shopping at a regional supermarket and received coupons in the mail that had nothing to do with my purchases whatsoever. Yet, I was using their mobile app and rewards number at every checkout. As a marketer, I knew immediately that the customer data collected on the backend wasn't being leveraged as best as it could be. Well, at least not to benefit customers at that moment in time. It upset me and frankly didn't entice me to keep shopping there as much. I didn't care to go out of my way to shop there, you know? Here I was handing out all my information and shopping insights for no value in return. If I'm giving you my information, I want you to use it to my benefit, too. Please. Sometime later, things changed for the better. I started to receive personalized coupons in the mail. Finally! It might seem minor, but it made all the difference. The value I received was personal to me and justified my continued spending there. Research shows that customers who take advantage of personalized offers end up spending more.[10] It's a good reminder that loyalty programs should start with the customer experience in mind and then move on to personalizing offers.[11] Just like Kroger managed to do successfully by creating quarterly, uniquely designed coupons for every household where 80 percent of the coupons are focused on personalizing the experience based on what the customer already likes and 20 percent on discovery efforts.[12] This coupon effort alone has generated $10 billion in revenue for Kroger.[13] No big deal.

All in all, the focus on personalization in reward or loyalty programs allows brands to build more meaningful connections that can help to attract, engage, and retain customers by tailoring their experiences. Still, that's not all there is to a successful program. Loyalty is won by delivering a superior customer experience consistently and providing new and innovative rewards and products. Whether you measure your success with levels of retention, reviews, repeat business, sentiment, interaction, frequency, or point programs, when you have something great, the right people will stand (and stay) behind your brand.

Love Notes

1. **Create superior customer experience**
   The right customer experience has a direct impact on the growth of your business. With the right customer service, you're more likely to have a satisfied customer that you can retain and who will promote you to others.
2. **Tell your story everywhere**
   Your story is a powerful way to connect and consumers want to know the story behind your brand. Remember, stories build emotional connections. Think about a coherent way to tell your story and find ways to tell it across all of your consumer touchpoints consistently, so you are relatable and personable to others.
3. **Be quick and simple**
   Convenience is a great value-add that can encourage consumers to spend (more) money with you. Figure out ways you can offer convenient options that save people time.

4 **Don't reinvent the wheel**
Innovation can start with brands or people. Many of the innovations that exist in today's world are things we didn't know we needed. How can you fill a consumer need that went unfulfilled before? You don't have to reinvent the wheel to be innovative. Find ways to do it better.

5 **Build loyalty**
With a rewards or loyalty program, you're able to deliver a valuable and personalized customer experience that extends beyond a purchase. Focus on the customer experience first by analyzing existing data. You can then leverage data to develop personalized benefits and perks to engage and retain your customer base.

PART FOUR
Love reinforced

11 Love brand lockdown

The "Brand Love Drivers" I shared in Chapter 1 show that brand love is a combination of both emotional and rational drivers. It's not one or the other. It's both. While function may pave the way for a company to gain success, emotional features are what keep the brand alive and fresh, giving consumers plenty of reason to stay connected beyond periods of time when they only "need" your product or service.

When a brand makes their audience feel seen and heard, the consumer-brand connection continues to grow stronger. As a brand, you prioritize seeing the world not only through your own eyes, but also through your audience's eyes. In a global crisis, such as the COVID-19 pandemic, brands will either enjoy the benefits of already being an emotionally engaged brand or start to build closeness with their customers. During periods of social or public turmoil, consumers are more likely to seek comfort from the products created by their favorite brands. Relationships that are more stable lead the way in times of challenge.

"Empathy" seems to be the new "relevance" when we look at important brand factors. Brands who show they "get you" and "feel you" can create marketing that means something. Like the time Delta Airlines threw a pizza party for passengers when their flight was delayed or canceled, creating feelings of joy and excitement as people started sharing pictures and posts on social media.[1] When you approach your consumers amid a current event, the message you send becomes more important than usual. As a brand, you have a unique opportunity to create relatable and relevant content in challenging times, and consumers are often ready and able to pay close attention to what brands are doing. Your goal should be to make every moment count.

COVID-19 led to lockdowns and travel restrictions, and standard consumer behavior was instantly impacted. This also created a variance in the way consumers were engaging with brands. The stressful period gave consumers even more reason to ask themselves: Is this purchase necessary? Consumers didn't necessarily stop spending money, but consider what you went through during this time. You were likely more cautious of, and intentional with, decisions surrounding where to spend your money. Within my own personal network, I noticed that many friends gravitated toward brands and products that allowed them to turn off or away from reality, because they wanted to fill their thoughts with things and brands who delivered experiences that didn't remind them of their current reality. Many friends spent time fixing their homes because they were spending more time there, and others baked their way through the discomfort of lockdown. And as it relates to baking, I was one of them. Baking provided feelings of comfort even though I had never spent much time doing it. Not only did it make me feel comfortable, but it also allowed me to create something tangible, which made my results-driven brain feel productive.

Given the circumstances, according to Talkwalker, people also relied more on online shopping, for instance, and started focusing on infotainment—casually consuming content that combines information/news and entertainment value.[2] Online platforms like YouTube helped to inform and entertain their audiences and therefore saw an increase in consumer use as well as brand content creation.[3] In addition to distraction from the situation, consumers also sought brands who provided comfort—emotional reassurance during a difficult time, according to the same research.[4] In times like this, human nature demands reassurance that everything is going to be alright. We want to know we're not alone on this journey. Changing consumer behavior redefines the digital conversations that take place, which include the topics that brands were discussing and the channels in which they were engaging.[5]

I'm not trying to pretend like the pandemic only had positive effects on brands. Though many brands used this opportunity to better understand and connect with their consumers, some weren't as fortunate to thrive, let alone survive as a business—whether big or small. One major industry to see huge effects was the hospitality industry. Decisions to shut down hotels, restaurants, and movies, let alone the limitations to travel, all had a negative impact. When we are faced with a changing ecosystem around us, we, as consumers, tick differently. Consumer behavior changes as a natural result and so does the way we engage with brands compared to "normal" times. If brands want to continue to be successful in the long term, they have no choice but to adjust alongside ever-changing consumer needs.

Global crisis: brand love stronger—or not

As I'm writing this, the pandemic has held its stance for almost three years now. This global disruption has affected almost every brand you can think of in either positive or negative ways, perhaps even both. But it has also provided great opportunities to strengthen brands through engagement, empathy, and meaningful connections. Understanding how consumer needs and wants change during hard times, and adapting to an evolving environment, shows that brands can continue to be relevant and optimize their future success.

What we can recognize during this time, too, are the brands who may not have been a so-called "love brand," but were able to launch into one for the simple reason that consumer demand transformed the need for certain categories. Household brands like Febreze and Charmin, both P&G brands, made it into the top 50 brands when they likely wouldn't have, considering their pre-pandemic "love levels," according to an article by WARC.[6]

Never in a million years did I think we would experience a shortage of toilet paper let alone see people hoarding it with their panic purchases. It makes sense to me that products like face masks and hand sanitizers would be sold out, and perhaps hoarded a little more. But toilet paper? A product that has an abundance of supply? Brands who are able to keep up with demand, like Charmin, and alleviate stress and anxiety for consumers who fear access to or supply of a product that we need in our everyday lives, seem to make people feel safe and secure. And brands or retailers who couldn't keep up with demand were simply replaced with other options. McKinsey & Company identified a trend as part of U.S. consumer sentiment and behavior during this time, showing that only 13 percent were patient enough to wait for an item to be in stock again compared to the 39 percent who switched brand or products, while 32 percent switched to a different retailer altogether, affecting brand loyalty.[7]

However, challenging economic times like this aren't only about consumers seeking the right brands to fulfill their needs and make them feel comfortable. Consumers also pay close attention to how companies treat their employees. Why? Because consumers choose brands who reflect good behavior everywhere. With the economy impacted across the world, it creates a pressing need for organizations to rethink and reconfigure their businesses on every level. To grow, they need to reinvent marketing and sales in a way that makes sense for consumers beyond their transactions.

The need for human touch

Businesses of all sizes experience disruptions. We saw this with the pandemic. It's true that larger businesses have more access to resources, which makes things easier. However, size doesn't always guarantee accuracy. Companies who know how to adapt and continuously provide value to their consumers rise above and beyond in tough times.

Just as we saw with Patagonia's 2011 "Don't buy this jacket" ad, the brands in lockdown had to get creative by advertising in totally new ways. Brands who know how to think on their feet can win the hearts of consumers. Specific to COVID-19, the brands who got creative with advertising and branding during lockdown were automotive brands such as Detroit's Big Three—General Motors, Ford, and Stellantis (formerly Fiat Chrysler Automobiles)—among other automotive suppliers that started producing ventilators and face masks because of a critical shortage across the world.[8] The technology platform Uber, known for transportation services, urged millions of riders to stay home with their Wieden + Kennedy campaign, "Thank

You For Not Riding."[9] Can you believe it? A company who moves people asked people not to move. How can you advise people not to do something if that action is a significant reason you exist at all? Efforts or campaigns such as this can make consumers feel like the brand truly cares on a deeper level.

During a time when human touch was literally taken away during the lockdown, moments such as with this campaign can make us feel connected again in different ways—through words, actions, and feelings that we are in this together as a community. Alone together. I'm not saying the lack of real human touch can be replaced in this way but the connection that made people feel close during what was mandatory isolation in most areas of the world, made a difference. I continue hearing people say how even with the simplicity of connecting with people virtually, the need for human connection can't be replaced. It's just not the same. We thrive on human connection that we feel through in-person interactions. We seek to love and be loved.

Audi, the automotive manufacturer and subsidiary of Volkswagen Group, introduced a personal experience to shoppers and owners during the COVID-19 lockdown. As events and shows were canceled throughout the world and Audi was unable to participate in brand activations to activate their vehicles for test drives, they pivoted by bringing the experience to your door, literally, for any service required.[10] In partnership with their participating Audi dealerships, "Audi at Your Door" was designed to provide an online shopping experience, one that was on the consumer's own terms.[11] This example from Audi highlights their ability to adapt when faced with changing consumer behavior.

People were accustomed to preparing meals in the comfort of their own home when they were encouraged to stay at home during the pandemic. A creative way to engage your audience makes sense, especially when it sparks a social media movement with lots of user-generated content. Brands like Burger King France provided their customers with the list of ingredients using store-bought items to make a home version of the Whopper, naming it "Quarantine Whopper" or in French, "Le Whopper de la Quarantine."[12] Announced on Twitter, this effort to give back and engage with their customer base was a big hit for the fast-food chain.[13] So much so that customers asked for recipes of other burgers that the chain provided.[14] During a time when eating out was not as easy for many individuals around the world, having a chance to replicate comfort foods in their own kitchens using easy-to-follow recipes and images that share instructions was a simple yet thoughtful and fun effort.

The right brands know how to act and position themselves during challenging times to continue to provide the right value. When you know what your customers need and deliver on it at the right time, you feed into the comfort they seek in that moment in time.

Function versus emotion

Zoom became the go-to video conferencing tool during the COVID-19 lockdown when live events started to get canceled and people began to work from home. It's interesting to observe how a brand like Zoom became so successful in such a short amount of time. But to be fair, the brand was already an established company with an infrastructure in place that continued to improve as customer use grew.

People quickly started sending Zoom invites for virtual events, parties, networking calls, baby showers, happy hours, and more. While there have always been other notable video meeting platforms in the market, before you knew it, Zoom's growth was so crazy that it quickly morphed into both a household name and a verb in our everyday language.

Usually, brands who attain a verb-ification status have become so common in daily use that you'd think they've attained the love brand status: "Can someone grab me a *Kleenex*?" or "This looks *photoshopped*." In this case, Kleenex has become synonymous with tissues and Photoshop has replaced reference to any software with this functionality, both denoting the power of brands. Other phrases or terms quickly became part of our daily vocabulary too, such as "I'm zoomed out" or "Zoom fatigue," explaining the feeling of tiredness and exhaustion after utilizing the platform too much. The brand also faced challenges during its peak time when users became concerned about security issues and privacy while using the platform, many of which have been fixed over time with two-factor authorization and enhanced encryption of meeting invites.

During such a relevant time in history, a brand can drive significant change in how we communicate and operate, even take over market share, yet have few emotions tied to it for some people. Despite the excessive use of the Zoom platform overall, people shared their thoughts about the brand: marketing executive Musa Tariq tweeted, "I think about the fact that I've used Zoom so much this year, had my son's 2nd birthday on it, experienced a friend's wedding, connected with old and new friends, did a yoga class on it, traveled the world through it and yet have 0 feelings about the brand."[15] Perhaps because it's so functional in nature, unlike a brand like TikTok that's tied to more emotions.

Does this mean that brands don't have to have emotional drivers to be successful? Not really. When products are so functional in nature and make it harder to attach emotional values, many times the value of people connecting or building a community because of the product's existence allows brands to build feelings around their products, too. The process is not always linear. Remember, "The Eight Brand Love Stages" and "Brand Love Drivers" indicate what your brand needs to develop a strong emotional and healthy consumer-brand connection.

Love Notes

1 **Make every moment count**
During challenging and difficult times, it pays to use moment marketing more than ever. You have to act quickly to understand your consumers' feelings in the moment. Think of ways to deliver relevant and relatable content.

2 **Turn empathy into action**
Consumers want brands to make their lives better. To do this, it's important to understand and connect with their emotions. When they feel heard and seen, you're both winning. So, focus on brand empathy first, conversions second.

3 **Embrace emotion**
Sometimes it's possible to build brands based mainly on function, but to build long-lasting, successful brands, you have to build in emotional drivers from day one. Be worthy of connecting with on a deeper emotional level.

Conclusion

I began the book by talking about the fact that we as people connect with brands the same way we connect with people, and I want to end the book with the fact that brands evolve like humans. As brand marketers, we develop brand identities to last for decades, but it remains true that building a brand is an ongoing process. As consumer needs and wants change, we learn the ways in which we, too, have to adapt to meet them where they are in their customer journey. The same is true for our brand offerings to ensure brand relevance and consistent value. Considering the plethora of choices that exist in today's world, you must continuously evolve your brand to be in service to your customers and give them a reason to not fall out of love with you.

The difference is between making a decision with your head or heart. In matters of love, we are told to follow our heart but to also listen to our head for the ultimate balance.

To take your customers on a long-lasting journey that sparks loyalty and advocacy, it's important to understand that brand love goes beyond customer infatuation and likeness. We know now that the same applies to consumer-brand connections. From the outset, we know how emotional benefits drive brand love. After this deep dive, we know how important the rational drivers are as well. Building a brand is no walk in the park but it's very rewarding when you do it the right way. As you continue your journey as a brand leader or marketer, I encourage you to think about ways you can foster both driver categories. Sure, this can be challenging but that's why I've given you this guide. Between "The Eight Brand Love Stages" model and "Brand Love Drivers," you now have what you need to make a difference in the consumer-brand journey and inspire emotion at every stage. Each one of these stages is as important as the other, and keeping nuance in mind as you continue will enable ample opportunities for consumers to have a holistic, emotional experience across the board.

Brand love looks different for everyone. It's your job to find what works for your customers, and the best way to do this is by going back to why you started in the first place. That's why we spent so much time in the book focusing on the importance of brand purpose. To reiterate: Focus on what you're selling at the core and why you exist as a brand.

A brand is more than a name, more than a mission or vision statement. A brand is an opportunity to connect and engage with individuals across different touchpoints to prove your value. Consumers are different yet wish for the same. They seek brands who provide peace of mind—the ones who provide comfort, happiness, and satisfaction. Consumers seek brands who provide more than a transaction. They want brands who represent something bigger and meaningful because to them, supporting a brand reflects who they are—it's a statement. They want to build a relationship with you beyond the coffee you're giving them to drink or the car you want them to drive. Yet, as humans, we want brands to cater to us as individuals, as *unique individuals*, because every human being has different goals and motivations. And as a brand, you should choose to be the one who's more human. Why? Because that's how emotional bonds are created. How? By being authentic and building a brand who is honest, true, and transparent. Tap into people's senses to create emotional and memorable experiences time and time again. Tell stories that are relatable and resonate well with others. *Brand love* is the way to go because experiences become more than just a memory; experiences become feelings. And feelings can turn into long-term loyalty and advocacy.

After all, emotional marketing is about creating desire for your brand and learning how to create an intimate relationship with your audience where you can play an active role in their lives every day. In a way, a brand gives consumers an opportunity to ultimately identify with the brand and build long-lasting trust and affinity—just like "The Eight Brand Love Stages" indicate. Keeping up with consumers might not always be easy and straightforward, but the best brands are the ones who know who they are at their core and deliver experiences to meet consumers where they are through the different stages in their lives. They find ways to cater to consumers in the right fashion by connecting with their shared values. As the role of brand evolves, I believe the future will only focus on more emotion and humanization of brands to grow closer to their consumer base and drive success. There's little denying that these brands pave the way to revenue growth and profit.

In the end, the brands who remind us of their unique value and bring out the best in us, inspire us to be better versions of ourselves. They make the world we live in a better place as we embark on this journey together.

ACKNOWLEDGMENTS

It takes many people to create a great story let alone a first book. With the help and kindness of many people, this book came to fruition in ways I couldn't have imagined. I'm so grateful to everyone who was a part of this special journey in my life and the ones I met throughout this process. My first big thank you goes to my acquisitions editor Bronwyn Geyer at Kogan Page, who reached out to me to get this journey started as she saw a book worth writing. I appreciate your continuous encouragement, support, editing, and fine-tuning throughout the process. You pushed me to write from my own point of view and showed me the importance of including my own voice throughout the book. Oscar Spigolon, you crushed the book cover design! I appreciate your patience in bringing my creative vision to life. I'm also thankful to the rest of the Kogan Page team in London and New York that includes Vanessa Rueda, Theresa Personna, Ed Kos, Bruna Sperotto, Donna Goddard, and Nancy Wallace. This process has been such a great learning experience!

Writing my first book wasn't easy but as with everything in life, I learned that with the right help and support system everything is possible. I wrote this book during an eventful year to say the least. It was a rewarding journey that allowed me to pour out my research, thoughts and experiences I've accumulated over the years. I knew that a book on *brand love* would demand closeness and vulnerability, so sharing this side of me along with some of my personal experiences pushed me to open up in a way I had never done before.

Thank you to my clients at Blended Collective, who showed their trust by working with me on their brand development and marketing process. Justin Summerville from Mayfield Athletics, Aisha Blake and Benjamin Lippi from Opal Grove Games, and Bass Paulus from Fusion Epicure—keep thriving! Allowing me to share your projects and stories with others in this way means a lot. And a special thank you to my team and multicultural advisory board at Blended Collective: Kevin Ketels, Randall McAdory, Brenda Marshall, and

Ceyla Özdemir. Your positivity and excitement for my first book inspired me to keep going even when it was challenging at times.

I also want to recognize the business owners, marketers, brand and creative leaders who took time to be interviewed to add more depth to the examples and stories I chose to share to enrich this book: James Gregson from The LEGO Group, Steve Keller from Studio Resonate/SXM Media, Kevin Peterson from Sfumato Fragrances and Castalia, and Fares Ksebati from MySwimPro. I'm thankful for the conversations we had throughout this process and to experience your passion for the work you do.

I'm also grateful for the companies who granted permission to use their copyrighted works: Talkwalker, Edelman, Escalent, McKinsey & Company, Nielsen, Porsche Consulting, Simon-Kucher & Partners, Association of National Advertisers (ANA), L'Oréal Deutschland (Germany), True Fruits, HARIBO, Huda Beauty, Chobani, Warby Parker, Patagonia, Ben & Jerry's, Dove, Toyota, Peloton, Tom Peters Company, Detroit Symphony Orchestra, Takoi, Connection Builders, and Townsquare Media (thank you for your letter, Christine!). Next, I can't forget the brands who were kind enough to share input about content that mentions them: Mastercard, TOMS, and KFC. And thanks to WARC for providing me with access to your suite of content during my time of writing.

I want to be mindful of the individuals who contributed to this journey and book by sharing feedback or insights throughout this process: Musa Tariq, Jon Freshwater, Ashmi Elizabeth Dang, Ashley Williams, and Annick Busch. Much love Ziad, Jayden, and Brooklyn—thank you for participating in the selection of my book cover and sharing your excitement with me. A special thank you to Chris Barr for designing the figure for the "Brand Love Drivers." You've been a great collaborator over the years, and I appreciate your creativity! Thank you, Dr. Stoltman, for your time to contribute to the framing of the book and brand love model, ensuring a cohesive flow and meaning all around. And thank you Sherry Cummins, Franziska Hildebrandt, and Kevin Ketels for reading an early draft of the chapters to provide additional insights, feedback, and improvements to make this book as great as possible.

Without the support of my parents, my sister Tanja, and my friends (you know who you are) who believed in me at every step of the way and shared words of encouragement throughout the entire process, this book wouldn't have been possible. Thank you for putting up with me during this arduous writing process.

Finally, I dedicate this book to my dear godmother Tante Helga. You are the epitome of what it means to be an authentic human in the kindest way possible. You exemplify love in everything you do. I am *forever* inspired.

Notes

Introduction

1 Reproduced with permission of Porsche Consulting ©2021. "The Secret of Love" www.porsche-consulting.com/fileadmin/docs/04_Medien/Publikationen/829377_The_Secret_of_Love/The_Secret_of_Love_2021_C_Porsche_Consulting.pdf (archived at https://perma.cc/RNX4-C6ZT)

2 Reproduced with permission of Tom Peters Company. Appears in Joachimsthaler, E and Aaker, D A (2012) *Brand Leadership*, United Kingdom: Simon & Schuster UK, p 16

Chapter 1

1 Kübler-Ross, E and Kessler, D (2012) *Life Lessons: Two experts on death and dying teach us about the mysteries of life and living*, United States: Scribner. Page 118.

2 Adapted with Permission from Talkwalker, SARL. © 2021. "Brand Love Story," www.talkwalker.com/resource/report/love-brand-report-eng-2021-final.pdf (archived at https://perma.cc/Z2LW-3HUS)

3 Ibid.

4 Ibid.

5 Copyrighted Information © (2021) of the Nielsen Company, licensed for use herein. "Inclusion, Information, and Intersection. The truth about connecting with U.S. Latinos," www.nielsen.com/wp-content/uploads/sites/2/2021/09/nielsen-2021-hispanic-diverse-insights-report-210682-D9.pdf (archived at https://perma.cc/WH6N-56P5)

6 Ibid.

7 Adapted with permission of Daniel J. Edelman Holdings, Inc. © 2021. "2021 Edelman Trust Barometer Special Report: Trust, The new brand equity," www.edelman.com/trust/2021-brand-trust/brand-equity (archived at https://perma.cc/8M6C-X9AD)

8 NPR (2008) "Assisted Listen: Erykah Badu's 'New Amerykah'," *NPR*, 14 April www.npr.org/2008/04/14/89612863/assisted-listen-erykah-badus-new-amerykah (archived at https://perma.cc/J9ZR-EDE5)

9 Lombrozo, T (2013) "The truth about the left brain/right brain relationship," *NPR*, 2 December, www.npr.org/sections/13.7/2013/12/02/248089436/the-truth-about-the-left-brain-right-brain-relationship (archived at https://perma.cc/BH7B-S4WG)

10 Groth, A (2012) "You're the average of the five people you spend the most time with," *Business Insider*, 24 July, www.businessinsider.com/jim-rohn-youre-the-average-of-the-five-people-you-spend-the-most-time-with-2012-7 (archived at https://perma.cc/RUQ3-8UXL)

Chapter 2

1 Language used with permission from Mayfield Athletics.

2 Adapted with permission of Blended Collective © 2022. "Mayfield Athletics," www.blendedcollective.com/mayfield-athletics/ (archived at https://perma.cc/9FGP-7P75).

3 Adapted with permission of L'Oréal Deutschland GmbH © 2022. "Create the beauty that moves the world," www.loreal.com/de-de/germany/ (archived at https://perma.cc/KUB8-A6V2)

4 L'Oréal © 2022. "Our global brands portfolio," www.loreal.com/en/our-global-brands-portfolio/ (archived at https://perma.cc/7NHU-WBED)

5 Ibid.

6 Mintel (2021) "US marketing to Millennials market report 2021," store.mintel.com/report/us-marketing-to-millennials-market-report (archived at https://perma.cc/5G8W-APB4)

7 Destatis (2023) "Bevölkerungsstand: Amtliche Einwohnerzahl Deutschlands 2022," www.destatis.de/DE/Themen/Gesellschaft-Umwelt/Bevoelkerung/Bevoelkerungsstand/_inhalt.html (archived at https://perma.cc/7D7H-S3CQ)

8 Businesswire (2022) "DIOR Beauty launch industry-first WhatsApp campaign with global influencer Jisoo," www.businesswire.com/news/home/20220509005205/en/DIOR-Beauty-Launch-Industry-First-WhatsApp-Campaign-With-Global-Influencer-Jisoo (archived at https://perma.cc/UWB3-QSQ7)

9 Adapted with permission of L'Oréal Deutschland GmbH © 2022. "Entdecke Fructis," www.garnier.de/haarpflege/haarpflege-marken/fructis (archived at https://perma.cc/6YSG-RJ4T)

Chapter 3

1 Cătălin, M and Andreea, P (2014) "Brands as a Mean of Consumer Self-expression and Desired Personal Lifestyle," *Procedia – Social and Behavioral Sciences*, **109**, p 104, www.sciencedirect.com/science/article/pii/S1877042813050593?ref=pdf_download&fr=RR-2&rr=73de1e49de602ca1 (archived at https://perma.cc/4ZZ5-ZUHP)

2 Ibid.

3 Adapted with permission of Huda Beauty © 2022. Huda Beauty Instagram, www.instagram.com/hudabeauty/?hl=en (archived at https://perma.cc/V5UM-8WRX)

4 Reproduced with permission of Huda Beauty © 2022. "About us," hudabeauty.com/default/aboutus.html (archived at https://perma.cc/GG7W-SUZ2)

5 Adapted with permission of Huda Beauty © 2022. "About Wishful," hudabeauty.com/us/en_US/aboutwishful.html (archived at https://perma.cc/R3NK-3XZB)

6 Adapted with permission of Huda Beauty © 2022. "Wishful is about to change your skin forever," hudabeauty.com/us/en_US/blog-wishful-skincare-by-huda-kattan-66410.html (archived at https://perma.cc/K23J-GPXV)

7 Adapted with permission of Dove © 2023. "Welcome to the Dove Self-Esteem Project," www.dove.com/us/en/dove-self-esteem-project.html?gclid=EAIaIQobChMI_oj7q-yp-gIVJIdbCh1ULwP5EAAYASAAEgI9TfD_BwE&gclsrc=aw.ds (archived at https://perma.cc/Z9Q9-6N67)

8 Adapted with permission of Dove © 2023. "About Dove," www.dove.com/us/en/stories/about-dove.html (archived at https://perma.cc/6HK7-P32N)

9 Adapted with permission of Dove. © 2023. "Welcome to the Dove Self-Esteem Project." www.dove.com/us/en/dove-self-esteem-project.html?gclid=EAIaIQobChMI_oj7q-yp-gIVJIdbCh1ULwP5EAAYASAAEgI9TfD_BwE&gclsrc=aw.ds (archived at https://perma.cc/RJ2X-68AU)

10 Ibid.

11 Ibid.

12 Adapted with permission of Dove © 2023. "Help your child develop a positive body image," www.dove.com/us/en/dove-self-esteem-project/help-for-parents/talking-about-appearance/positive-body-image.html (archived at https://perma.cc/9LY2-RW89)

13 Ibid.

14 IPA (2022) "Sainsbury's: How an idea helped make Sainsbury's great again," ipa.co.uk/knowledge/case-studies/sainsbury-s-how-an-idea-helped-make-sainsbury-s-great-again (archived at https://perma.cc/CV4N-ZQ44)

15 Ibid.

16 National Projections (2014) "Projecting Majority-Minority, United States Census Bureau," www.census.gov/content/dam/Census/newsroom/releases/2015/cb15-tps16_graphic.pdf (archived at https://perma.cc/GNJ4-7LNS)

17 Copyrighted Information © (2022) of the Nielsen Company, licensed for use herein. "Confronting myth & marginalization. Asian American audiences and on-screen representation," www.nielsen.com/about-us/diversity-equity-inclusion/asian-american/ (archived at https://perma.cc/6XSH-CQCF)

18 Ibid.

19 Ibid.

20 Copyrighted Information © (2021) of the Nielsen Company, licensed for use herein. "Seeing and believing: Meeting Black audience demand for representation that matters," www.nielsen.com/insights/2021/seeing-and-believing-meeting-black-audience-demand-for-representation-that-matters/ (archived at https://perma.cc/N6KC-5LNL)

21 Copyrighted Information © (2022) of the Nielsen Company, licensed for use herein. Graham, K (2022) "Black consumers empowered by 'selfless' spending," Nielsen, 9 February, nielseniq.com/global/en/insights/analysis/2022/black-consumers-empowered-by-selfless-spending/ (archived at https://perma.cc/D39F-E64K)

22 Copyrighted Information © (2021) of the Nielsen Company, licensed for use herein. "Seeing and believing: Meeting Black audience demand for representation that matters," www.nielsen.com/insights/2021/seeing-and-believing-meeting-black-audience-demand-for-representation-that-matters/ (archived at https://perma.cc/UXG9-EYXZ)

23 Copyrighted Information © (2022) of the Nielsen Company, licensed for use herein. "Hispanic Representation," www.nielsen.com/about-us/diversity-equity-inclusion/hispanic/ (archived at https://perma.cc/4EYD-9GN9)

24 Copyrighted Information © (2021) of the Nielsen Company, licensed for use herein. "Being seen on screen: The importance of quantity and quality representation on TV," www.nielsen.com/insights/2021/being-seen-on-screen/ (archived at https://perma.cc/W6GX-M6HD)

25 Marc, F and Patrick, S (2017) "True Fruits: A Juiced-Up Internationalization Strategy." Harvard Business Publishing, www.hbsp.harvard.edu/product/W17689-PDF-ENG (archived at https://perma.cc/33YU-XFKT)

26 Adapted with permission of True Fruits © 2022. www.instagram.com/truefruitssmoothies/?hl=en (archived at https://perma.cc/MW8Y-KJMT)

27 Adapted with permission of True Fruits © 2022. "flaschenaufsätze," true-fruits.com/flaschenaufsaetze/ (archived at https://perma.cc/K2NS-MGEX)

28 Lindt USA (2013) "Say HELLO to a new sweet and stylish premium chocolate collection from Lindt," *Cision PR Newswire*, www.prnewswire.com/news-releases/say-hello-to-a-new-sweet-and-stylish-premium-chocolate-collection-from-lindt-212766691.html (archived at https://perma.cc/NY4E-NESV)

29 Ibid.

30 Ibid.

31 Ibid.

32 Kiefer, B (2022) "Why British Airways created more than 500 unique ads to restore brand love," *AdWeek*, 24 October, www.adweek.com/creativity/why-british-airways-created-more-than-500-unique-ads-to-restore-brand-love/ (archived at https://perma.cc/FF2R-VDKT)

33 Melody Ehsani (2022) "Accessories," melodyehsani.com/collections/candles (archived at https://perma.cc/HZT8-MSVK)

34 The Hundreds (2022) Email subscription "The Hundreds"

35 Ibid.

36 Ibid.

Chapter 4

1 Reproduced with permission of Peloton © 2022. "The Peloton Story," www.onepeloton.com/company (archived at https://perma.cc/6KKG-TJVF)

2 Reproduced with permission of Connection Builders © 2021. "Taking control of your personal brand – Lydia Michael," Branch Out Podcast – Episode 74, 8 February 2022, open.spotify.com/episode/4op3wMa57zNdM05TWx8x1f (archived at https://perma.cc/EA9A-6HBS)

3 Adapted with permission of Escalent © 2020. "Brand Authenticity: What it means, why it matters and how to get there," landing.escalent.co/download-brand-authenticity-what-it-means-why-it-matters-and-how-to-get-there (archived at https://perma.cc/VJS4-9JSS)

4 Ibid.

5 Ibid.

6 Ibid.

7 Ibid.

8 Ibid.

9 Ibid.

10 Ibid.

11 Christine (2021) "A love letter to Trader Joe's on 'Christine-ology'," Mix 95.7 West Michigan, 29 April, www.mix957gr.com/a-love-letter-to-trader-joes-on-christine-ology/ (archived at https://perma.cc/UK7T-QELX) Used with permission.

12 Chernev, A, Böckenholt, U and Goodman, J (2015) "Choice overload: A conceptual review and meta-analysis," *Journal of Consumer Psychology*, 25 (2), pp 333–58, www.sciencedirect.com/science/article/abs/pii/S1057740814000916 (archived at https://perma.cc/KAU6-6E97)

13 Adapted with permission of Escalent © 2020. "Brand Authenticity: What it means, why it matters and how to get there," landing.escalent.co/download-brand-authenticity-what-it-means-why-it-matters-and-how-to-get-there (archived at https://perma.cc/TP7M-MYSD)

14 Ibid.

15 Brittany, W (2018) "Crowdsourcing your next chip flavor lays do us a flavor campaign," Harvard Business School, March 24, www.d3.harvard.edu/platform-digit/submission/crowdsourcing-your-next-chip-flavor-lays-do-us-a-flavor-campaign/ (archived at https://perma.cc/QHM6-S2NY)

16 Adapted with permission of Huda Beauty © 2020. Huda Beauty Instagram, www.instagram.com/tv/CAYZVDtjcCq/?igshid=YmMyMTA2M2Y%3D (archived at https://perma.cc/F47E-KYWH)

17 Ibid.

18 Ibid.

19 Ibid.

20 Ibid.

21 Ibid.

22 Ibid.

23 Adapted with permission of Talkwalker, SARL © 2022. "Love Brands. How sustainability builds love for today and the future," www.talkwalker.com/case-studies/brand-love-report (archived at https://perma.cc/KF5N-A7T9)

24 BBC (2018) "KFC's apology for running out of chicken is pretty cheeky," *BBC News*, 23 February, www.bbc.com/news/newsbeat-43169625 (archived at https://perma.cc/6QNN-3UZ8)

25 Ibid.

26 Ibid.

27 Ads of the World (2022) "The Moldy Whopper," www.adsoftheworld.com/campaigns/the-moldy-whopper (archived at https://perma.cc/SAA7-TZ9W)

28 Handley, L (2020) "Burger King's moldy Whopper ad is dividing marketing experts," *CNBC*, 24 February, www.cnbc.com/2020/02/20/burger-kings-moldy-whopper-ad-is-dividing-marketing-experts.html (archived at https://perma.cc/K244-X96Y)

29 Ibid.

30 Words included on a product label.

31 Bronner, S (2018) "The Founders of RXBar, acquired by Kellogg for $600 Million, built the company by 'having a bias toward action'," *Entrepreneur*, 29 January. www.entrepreneur.com/growing-a-business/the-founders-of-rxbar-acquired-by-kellogg-for-600/308136 (archived at https://perma.cc/R8SJ-87UU)

32 RXBAR (2022) "The RXBAR Story," www.rxbar.com/en_US/real-talk/articles/our-story.html (archived at https://perma.cc/E9Y6-W6YG)

33 Ibid.

34 Upham, B (2021) "Why are some food additives that are banned in Europe still used in the U.S.?" *Everyday Health*, 13 October, www.everydayhealth.com/diet-nutrition/why-are-some-food-additives-that-are-banned-in-europe-still-used-in-the-us/ (archived at https://perma.cc/USU3-JGQ7)

35 RXBAR (2022) "The RXBAR Story," www.rxbar.com/en_US/real-talk/articles/our-story.html (archived at https://perma.cc/E9Y6-W6YG)

36 Adapted with permission of Chobani © 2022. "About Chobani," www.chobani.com/about/ (archived at https://perma.cc/8JPL-JX96)

37 Ibid.

38 Reproduced with permission of Dove © 2023. "Let's Change Beauty," www.dove.com/us/en/stories/about-dove/change-beauty.html (archived at https://perma.cc/WX7Z-NKSM)

39 Ibid.

Chapter 5

1 Adapted with permission of Talkwalker, SARL © 2022. "Love Brands. How sustainability builds love for today and the future," www.talkwalker.com/case-studies/brand-love-report (archived at https://perma.cc/7NTS-PVY7)

2 Adapted with permission of Shikha Jain and Simon-Kucher & Partners © 2022. Jain, S and Hagenbeek, O, "2022 Global Sustainability Study: The growth potential of environmental change," www.simon-kucher.com/en/blog/2022-global-sustainability-study-growth-potential-environmental-change (archived at https://perma.cc/J7MY-A8BA)

3 Adapted with permission of Patagonia © 2022. "1% percent for the planet," www.patagonia.com/one-percent-for-the-planet.html (archived at https://perma.cc/K8XH-C25S)

4 Adapted with permission of Patagonia © 2022. "Company history," www.patagonia.com/company-history/ (archived at https://perma.cc/GSL8-FGJ6)

5 Adapted with permission of Patagonia © 2022. www.patagonia.com/home/ (archived at https://perma.cc/8WPD-C39R)

6 Allchin, J (2013) "Case study: Patagonia's 'Don't buy this jacket campaign'," *Marketing Week*, 23 January, www.marketingweek.com/case-study-patagonias-dont-buy-this-jacket-campaign/ (archived at https://perma.cc/TMZ2-7MJH)

7 Adapted with permission of Patagonia © 2022. "Exchanges, Returns & Repairs," www.patagonia.com/returns.html (archived at https://perma.cc/F3D5-NKQL)

8 Li, N (2022) "Bottega Veneta launches lifetime warranty for its bags," *Hypebeast*, 1 November, hypebeast.com/2022/11/bottega-veneta-bag-lifetime-warranty-launch-info (archived at https://perma.cc/HM48-X6LB)

9 Allchin, J (2013) "Case study: Patagonia's 'Don't buy this jacket campaign'," *Marketing Week*, 23 January, www.marketingweek.com/case-study-patagonias-dont-buy-this-jacket-campaign/ (archived at https://perma.cc/ZU7T-JKBT)

10 Ibid.

11 Adapted with permission of Patagonia © 2022. "Earth is now our only shareholder," www.patagonia.com/ownership/ (archived at https://perma.cc/74S2-D22Y)

12 "Ben & Jerry's is fighting for climate justice, one scoop at a time" on Ben & Jerry's website, www.benjerry.com/whats-new/2021/10/ben-jerrys-fighting-for-climate-justice (archived at https://perma.cc/B39Z-LA6Y)

13 Adapted with permission of Ben & Jerry's © 2022. "Our History," www.benjerry.com/about-us (archived at https://perma.cc/VP7Y-NQS9). Used with permission.

14 Reproduced with permission of Ben & Jerry's. © 2022, "We use our position to influence change," www.benjerry.com/values/issues-we-care-about (archived at https://perma.cc/7WN7-KVBB). Used with permission.

15 Adapted with permission of Ben & Jerry's © 2022. "Change is brewing, Ben & Jerry's," www.benjerry.com/flavors/change-is-brewing-ice-cream (archived at https://perma.cc/55X9-H9WG). Used with permission.

16 Adapted with permission of Ben & Jerry's © 2022. "Why we're rebranding a flavor to celebrate the power of black voters," www.benjerry.com/whats-new/2022/09/change-is-brewing (archived at https://perma.cc/72F7-WGSA). Used with permission.

17 Language used with permission from Ben & Jerry's.

18 Adapted with permission of Daniel J. Edelman Holdings, Inc. © 2019. "2019 Edelman Trust Barometer Special Report: In Brands We Trust?" www.edelman.com/research/trust-barometer-special-report-in-brands-we-trust (archived at https://perma.cc/4QNP-YH4N)

19 Adapted with permission of Daniel J. Edelman Holdings, Inc. © 2022. "2022 Edelman Trust Barometer," www.edelman.com/sites/g/files/aatuss191/files/2022-01/2022%20Edelman%20Trust%20Barometer%20FINAL_Jan25.pdf (archived at https://perma.cc/652M-BRJ8)

20 Ibid.

21 Tyson, A, and Kennedy, B and Funk, C (2021) "Gen Z, Millennials stand out for climate change activism, social media engagement with issue," *Pew Research*, 26 May, www.pewresearch.org/science/2021/05/26/gen-z-millennials-stand-out-for-climate-change-activism-social-media-engagement-with-issue/ (archived at https://perma.cc/9DWK-Z34B)

22 Zwieglinska, Z (2022) "How brands are tackling mental health to connect with younger customers," *Glossy*, 3 May, www.glossy.co/fashion/how-brands-are-tackling-mental-health-to-connect-with-younger-customers/ (archived at https://perma.cc/NJ2K-WYH7)

23 TOMS "In it for the long haul," www.toms.com/us/impact/planet.html (archived at https://perma.cc/WVU4-YDDS)

24 World Health Organization (2019) "WHO launches first World report on vision," World Health Organization, 8 October, www.who.int/news/item/08-10-2019-who-launches-first-world-report-on-vision (archived at https://perma.cc/YQ6K-4FG6)

25 Adapted with permission of Warby Parker © 2022 "Buy a pair, give a pair. The whole story begins with you," www.warbyparker.com/buy-a-pair-give-a-pair (archived at https://perma.cc/779Q-DLQ2)

26 Levy, S (2022) "CVS Health launches HERe, healthier happens together," drugstorenews.com/cvs-health-launches-here-healthier-happens-together (archived at https://perma.cc/QU8E-E8MC)

27 Ibid.

Chapter 6

1 Adapted with permission of Daniel J. Edelman Holdings, Inc. © (2022) "2022 Edelman Trust Barometer," www.edelman.com/sites/g/files/aatuss191/files/2022-01/2022%20Edelman%20Trust%20Barometer%20FINAL_Jan25.pdf (archived at https://perma.cc/DJ67-ZYYH)

2 Ibid.

3 Ibid.

4 Adapted with permission of Daniel J. Edelman Holdings, Inc. © (2019) "2019 Edelman Trust Barometer Special Report: In Brands We Trust?" www.edelman.com/research/trust-barometer-special-report-in-brands-we-trust (archived at https://perma.cc/8KV2-RE94)

5 Adapted with permission of Daniel J. Edelman Holdings, Inc. © (2022) "2022 Edelman Trust Barometer," www.edelman.com/sites/g/files/aatuss191/files/2022-01/2022%20Edelman%20Trust%20Barometer%20FINAL_Jan25.pdf (archived at https://perma.cc/Q7NH-QHH2)

6 Ibid.

7 Reproduced with permission of HARIBO © 2022. "Our values – unmistakably HARIBO, Happiness with responsibility," www.haribo.com/en-au/about-us/cr/values (archived at https://perma.cc/K5TW-ETKU)

8 Ibid.

9 HARIBO (2022) "HARIBO Releases New Flavors, Limited Edition Shapes for 100th Birthday of Iconic Goldbears Gummies," HARIBO, 1 January, www.haribo.com/en-us/news/haribo-releases-new-flavors-limited-edition-shapes-for-100th-birthday-of-iconic-goldbears-gummies (archived at https://perma.cc/28LW-TBE6)

10 Ibid.

11 Lewis, A (2021) "Orange twirls are here to stay thanks to Cadbury," *Delish*, 5 February, www.delish.com/uk/food-news/a35428498/orange-twirl/ (archived at https://perma.cc/6KRN-MAUY)

12 Reproduced with permission of HARIBO © 2022. "Our values – unmistakably HARIBO, Happiness with responsibility," www.haribo.com/en-au/about-us/cr/values (archived at https://perma.cc/9UMS-9QNB)

13 Ibid.

14 Perkins, T (2017) "Why Katoi is an offensive restaurant name and should be changed," *Detroit Metro Times*, 21 August, www.metrotimes.com/food-drink/why-katoi-is-an-offensive-restaurant-name-and-should-be-changed-5072744 (archived at https://perma.cc/K2WF-8H7L)

15 Kurlyandchik, M (2017) "In response to criticism, Corktown's Katoi restaurant gets new name," www.freep.com/story/entertainment/dining/mark-kurlyandchik/2017/08/23/katoi-detroit-changes-name-takoi-restaurant/594711001/ (archived at https://perma.cc/8Y3U-KDXS)

16 Adapted with permission of Takoi © 2022. www.takoidetroit.com/about (archived at https://perma.cc/3SVT-K5JV)

17 Oxford Reference (2022) "Cultural appropriation," www.oxfordreference.com/view/10.1093/oi/authority.20110803095652789 (archived at https://perma.cc/BT5F-P23E)

18 Adapted with permission of McKinsey & Company. © 2020. "Diversity Wins. How Inclusion Matters," www.mckinsey.com/~/media/mckinsey/featured%20insights/diversity%20and%20inclusion/diversity%20wins%20how%20inclusion%20matters/diversity-wins-how-inclusion-matters-vf.pdf (archived at https://perma.cc/X7Y8-54FD)

19 Adapted with permission of McKinsey & Company © 2022. "The rise of the inclusive consumer," February 8, www.mckinsey.com/industries/retail/our-insights/the-rise-of-the-inclusive-consumer (archived at https://perma.cc/7K6J-P3CV)

20 Ibid.

21 Target mobile app (2022).

22 Adapted with permission of McKinsey & Company © 2022. "The rise of the inclusive consumer," February 8, www.mckinsey.com/industries/retail/our-insights/the-rise-of-the-inclusive-consumer (archived at https://perma.cc/M2U3-VSYZ)

23 Adapted with permission of Association of National Advertisers. © 2022. "Supplier Diversity Resources," www.ana.net/content/show/id/supplierdiversity (archived at https://perma.cc/3QWF-8VST)

24 Language used with permission from Bill Duggan on December 14, 2022.

25 Ibid.

26 Morgan Stanley. "Multicultural Innovation Lab," www.morganstanley.com/about-us/diversity/multicultural-innovation-lab (archived at https://perma.cc/4DKH-A7SX)

Chapter 7

1 Reproduced with permission of MySwimPro, Inc. © 2022. myswimpro.com/about/ (archived at https://perma.cc/PK47-DAVK)

2 Reproduced with permission of MySwimPro, Inc. © 2022. blog.myswimpro.com/2021/11/11/meet-fares-ksebati-myswimpro-ceo-co-founder/ (archived at https://perma.cc/6A9E-V9SC)

3 Language used with permission following a conversation with Fares Ksebati on 5 January 2023.

4 Reproduced with permission of MySwimPro, Inc. © 2022. blog.myswimpro.com/2021/11/11/meet-fares-ksebati-myswimpro-ceo-co-founder/ (archived at https://perma.cc/V3AH-SJ2H)

5 Language used with permission following an interview conducted with Fares Ksebati on 10 February 2022.

6 Ibid.

7 Facebook (2023) "MySwimPro Global Community," www.facebook.com/groups/MySwimproGlobalCommunity/ (archived at https://perma.cc/ALR9-CSUQ)

8 Adapted with permission of MySwimPro, Inc. © 2022. blog.myswimpro.com/2021/11/11/meet-fares-ksebati-myswimpro-ceo-co-founder/ (archived at https://perma.cc/YD8P-G9ML)

9 Gatorade "Gx Sweat Patch," www.gatorade.com/gear/tech/gx-sweat-patch/2-pack (archived at https://perma.cc/NCZ8-95L9)

10 Mastercard (2022) "hi launches world's first NFT Customizable Card with Mastercard," www.mastercard.com/news/europe/en/newsroom/press-releases/en/2022/september-2022/hi-launches-world-s-first-nft-customizable-card-with-mastercard/ (archived at https://perma.cc/ZAA3-VVWM)

11 Adapted with permission of McKinsey & Company © 2019. Boudet, J, Gregg, B, Rathje, K, Stein, E and Vollhardt, K, "The future of personalization – and how to get ready for it," www.mckinsey.com/capabilities/growth-marketing-and-sales/our-insights/the-future-of-personalization-and-how-to-get-ready-for-it (archived at https://perma.cc/4Q8W-CDL2)

Chapter 8

1 Mastercard (2019) "Mastercard evolves its brand mark by dropping its name," www.mastercard.com/news/press/2019/january/mastercard-evolves-its-brand-mark-by-dropping-its-name/ (archived at https://perma.cc/GJ7V-YXYF)

2 Mastercard "Introducing the Touch Card," www.mastercard.us/en-us/personal/find-a-card/touchcard.html (archived at https://perma.cc/4KNX-7J57)

3 Mastercard (2019) "Mastercard Debuts PRICELESS – An international culinary collective bringing the world's finest dining and cocktail experiences to New York City," www.mastercard.com/news/press/2019/july/mastercard-debuts-priceless-an-international-culinary-collective-bringing-the-world-s-finest-dining-and-cocktail-experiences-to-new-york-city/ (archived at https://perma.cc/LL99-GCY8)

4 Mastercard (2022) "Mastercard launches its first-ever music album: Priceless," www.mastercard.com/news/press/2022/june/mastercard-launches-its-first-ever-music-album-priceless/ (archived at https://perma.cc/8756-KA2F)

5 Hirsch, Alan R (1990) "Preliminary Results of Olfaction Nike Study," note dated November 16, distributed by the Smell and Taste Treatment and Research Foundation, Ltd. Chicago, IL.

6 Ibid.

7 Handwerk, B (2017) "In some ways, your sense of smell is actually better than a dog's," *Smithsonian Magazine*, www.smithsonianmag.com/science-nature/you-actually-smell-better-dog-180963391/ (archived at https://perma.cc/N8WL-26SH)

8 Ibid.

9 Ibid.

10 Adapted with permission of Sfumato Fragrances © 2022. sfumatofragrances.com (archived at https://perma.cc/4CJN-J337)

11 Adapted with permission of Sfumato Fragrances © 2022. "The meaning of 'Sfumato'," sfumatofragrances.com/blogs/news/what-does-sfumato-mean (archived at https://perma.cc/M7SS-YHKS)

12 Language used with permission following an interview conducted with Kevin Peterson on February 10, 2022.

13 Reproduced with permission of Detroit Symphony Orchestra, Inc. © 2022. "Mission & History," www.dso.org/about-the-dso/our-history/mission (archived at https://perma.cc/K7PC-PKRT)

14 Adapted with permission of Detroit Symphony Orchestra, Inc. © 2019. "DSO NextGen presents Mysterium III: A multisensory performance experience at The Max," www.dso.org/watch-listen-and-connect/newsroom-2/dso-nextgen-presents-mysterium-iii-a-multisensory-performance-experience-at-the-max-may-23 (archived at https://perma.cc/S2VS-YHH2)

15 Ibid.

16 Language used with permission following an interview conducted with Kevin Peterson on February 10, 2022.

17 Ibid.

18 Language used with permission following an interview conducted with Steve Keller on October 28, 2022.

19 Ibid.

20 Ibid.

21 Ibid.

22 Ibid.

23 Ibid.

24 Material referenced with permission from Toyota.

25 Etherington, D (2017) "Toyota wants to get us truly crushing on cars," *TechCrunch*, 29 October, techcrunch.com/2017/10/29/toyota-wants-to-get-us-truly-crushing-on-cars/ (archived at https://perma.cc/JM7M-E5TL)

26 Toyota (2017) "Toyota Concept-i makes the future of mobility human," Toyota Newsroom, 4 January, pressroom.toyota.com/toyota-concept-i-future-of-mobility-human-ces-2017/ (archived at https://perma.cc/GH3M-QYP5) Used with permission.

27 Adapted with permission of Talkwalker, SARL © 2021. "Brand Love Story," www.talkwalker.com/resource/report/love-brand-report-eng-2021-final.pdf (archived at https://perma.cc/7CSN-YMDP)

28 Bekemeyer, J (2022) "Buick expands partnership with Reese Witherspoon's media company," *DBusiness*, 17 August, www.dbusiness.com/daily-news/buick-expands-partnership-with-reese-witherspoons-media-company/ (archived at https://perma.cc/NNL6-FPFL)

29 YouTube (2022) "Buick: 'Dream with Us' See Buick's electric future vision," Timestamp: 0:40 – 0:46. www.youtube.com/watch?v=5COoOn-6dRw (archived at https://perma.cc/JY67-A2XZ)

30 Bekemeyer, J (2022) "Buick expands partnership with Reese Witherspoon's media company," *DBusiness*, 17 August, www.dbusiness.com/daily-news/buick-expands-partnership-with-reese-witherspoons-media-company/ (archived at https://perma.cc/R7DH-3KCU)

31 YouTube (2020) "Lincoln Aviator: 2020 Aviator Compositions with Karriem Riggins | Lincoln," www.youtube.com/watch?v=TTzPO0EvUGc (archived at https://perma.cc/9Z2U-T578)

32 Ibid.

33 Meisenzahl, M (2021) "Burger King's nostalgic rebrand was a huge hit. 2 designers explain why it was a success," *Business Insider India*, 18 February, www.businessinsider.in/retail/news/burger-kings-nostalgic-rebrand-was-a-huge-hit-2-designers-explain-why-it-was-a-success-/articleshow/81095924.cms (archived at https://perma.cc/8QQP-SH2B)

34 Paris, M (2022) "McDonald's brings back Hamburglar and Grimace in happy meal throwback," *Bloomberg*, 27 September, www.bloomberg.com/news/articles/2022-09-27/mcdonalds-new-happy-meals-with-cactus-plant-flea-market-are-a-throwback?leadSource=uverify%20wall (archived at https://perma.cc/LE76-2RY2)

35 Ibid.

36 Ibid.

37 Ibid.

38 Talkwalker (2020) "Talkwalker reveals the world's most loved brands - helping marketers reposition themselves for the new normal," Talkwalker, June 16. www.prnewswire.com/news-releases/talkwalker-reveals-the-worlds-most-loved-brands---helping-marketers-reposition-themselves-for-the-new-normal-301077307.html (archived at https://perma.cc/6XJU-4SX6)

39 The LEGO Group (2022) "About us," www.lego.com/en-us/aboutus (archived at https://perma.cc/ETS4-SY7D)

40 Language used with permission following an interview conducted with James Gregson on January 26, 2022.

41 Ibid.

Chapter 9

1 Kahlil Gibran (2007) *The Collected Works, The Prophet*, 1923, Alfred A. Knopf, page 105.

2 Language used with permission from Opal Grove Games.

3 Ibid.

4 Facebook (2013) LÄRABAR, 4 April, www.facebook.com/Larabar/posts/so-what-it-is-the-proper-pronunciation-of-the-lara-in-larabar-ive-heard-it-said-/10151348106506994/# (archived at https://perma.cc/85JX-H5EE)

5 Wilson, M (2017) "The story behind the cult hit LaCroix label," *Fast Company*, 31 January, www.fastcompany.com/3067745/the-story-behind-the-cult-hit-la-croix-label (archived at https://perma.cc/LP2V-7BQ9)

6 Adapted with permission of Fusion Gourmet Foods © 2023.

7 Ibid.

8 Ibid.

9 Ibid.

10 Ibid.

11 Ibid.

Chapter 10

1 Shu, C (2017) "NYX Cosmetics, known for its 'digital-first' marketing strategy, launches its own app," *TechCrunch*, 14 September, techcrunch.com/2017/09/14/nyx-makeup-crew/ (archived at https://perma.cc/M8VC-59VE)

2 O'Connor, C (2016) "Banking on beauty: How Tony Ko built NYX Cosmetics into a $500 million brand," *Forbes*, 20 June, www.forbes.com/sites/clareoconnor/2016/06/01/toni-ko-nyx-cosmetics-loreal-sale-richest-women/?sh=188b57157d71 (archived at https://perma.cc/Q4YG-7CVN)

3 Davenport, E (2022) "Warby Parker opens 200th retail store in Union Square," *The Villager*, 16 December, www.amny.com/news/warby-parker-opens-200th-store-union-square/ (archived at https://perma.cc/8YBQ-CQF2)

4 Scott, C (2022) "Warby Parker, launched as an online disrupter, now bets big on bricks and mortar," *Wall Street Journal*, 17 March, www.wsj.com/articles/warby-parker-shares-slide-on-slower-revenue-forecast-11647526324 (archived at https://perma.cc/PC45-FKLW)

5 This quote is reproduced with permission from Warby Parker © 2022.

6 Ibid.

7 Reproduced with permission of Warby Parker © 2022. "History," www.warbyparker.com/history (archived at https://perma.cc/W9KP-5P9Y)

8 Lukpat, A (2022) "Fast Food: See the top drive-through chains ranked quickest to slowest," www.wsj.com/articles/fast-food-drive-through-chains-ranked-quickest-to-slowest-list-11665427830?no_redirect=true (archived at https://perma.cc/9R3D-2837)

9 Lucas, A (2021) "It's not your imagination: Restaurant drive-thrus are slower and less accurate," CNBC, 23 September, www.cnbc.com/2021/09/23/its-not-your-imagination-restaurant-drive-thrus-are-slower-and-less-accurate.html (archived at https://perma.cc/G2JU-PEX7)

10 Covello, L (2021) "Why personalization is the holy grail of loyalty," *Forbes*, 9 November, www.forbes.com/sites/forbestechcouncil/2021/11/09/why-personalization-is-the-holy-grail-of-loyalty/?sh=32433265e77c (archived at https://perma.cc/UX22-XDQS)

11 Black, K (2017) "Why customer loyalty programs are so important," *Forbes*, 13 September, www.forbes.com/sites/kpmg/2017/09/13/why-customer-loyalty-programs-are-so-important/?sh=10b993e12bd4 (archived at https://perma.cc/8UP6-29ET)

12 Groenfeldt, T (2013) "Kroger knows your shopping patterns better than you do," *Forbes*, 28 October, www.forbes.com/sites/tomgroenfeldt/2013/10/28/kroger-knows-your-shopping-patterns-better-than-you-do/?sh=113485df746a (archived at https://perma.cc/VH9S-RKZT)

13 Ibid.

Chapter 11

1 Lewis, S (2017) "Delta throws pizza party for stranded passengers," CNN, 6 April, www.cnn.com/2017/04/06/us/delta-delays-pizza-trnd (archived at https://perma.cc/U7RN-ZMAA)

2 Adapted with permission of Talkwalker, SARL © 2021. "Brand Love Story," www.talkwalker.com/resource/report/love-brand-report-eng-2021-final.pdf (archived at https://perma.cc/9T66-NYXY)

3 Ibid.

4 Ibid.

5 Ibid.

6 Sakal, V (2020) "How brand love fuels lower funnel KPIs, even during a pandemic," *WARC*, September, www.warc.com/content/paywall/article/warc-exclusive/how-brand-love-fuels-lower-funnel-kpis-even-during-a-pandemic/en-GB/133912? (archived at https://perma.cc/7RM4-KPE9)

7 Adapted with permission of McKinsey & Company © (2021). "US consumer sentiment and behaviors during the coronavirus crisis," www.mckinsey.com/capabilities/growth-marketing-and-sales/our-insights/survey-us-consumer-sentiment-during-the-coronavirus-crisis (archived at https://perma.cc/P4TN-4MGY)

8 Turner, G (2020) "The big three vs. COVID-19," *DBusiness*, 21 April, www.dbusiness.com/from-the-magazine/the-big-three-vs-covid-19/ (archived at https://perma.cc/H4MU-7JZ4)

9 Diaz, A (2020) "Uber thanks people for not riding with Uber," *AdAge*, 10 April, adage.com/creativity/work/uber-thank-you-not-riding/2249401 (archived at https://perma.cc/W5F9-ZFNZ)

10 Audi (2022) www.audiusa.com/us/web/en/shopping-tools/audi-at-your-door.html (archived at https://perma.cc/U9DR-2BKP)

11 Ibid.

12 The Drum (2022) "Burger King: Le whopper de la quarantine by Buzzman." www.thedrum.com/creative-works/project/buzzman-burger-king-le-whopper-de-la-quarantaine (archived at https://perma.cc/XU7Y-FN2M)

13 Ibid.

14 Ibid.

15 Musa Tariq, December 9, 2021. Text written by him and posted on personal Twitter page: @Musa. Used with permission.

INDEX